Used Timeshares

Used Timeshares - A Guide to Buying, Using, Exchanging,
Renting, and Disposing of Timeshares

Lee W. Lacy

Trafford Publishing

Order this book online at www.trafford.com
or email orders@trafford.com

Most Trafford titles are also available at major online book retailers.

Printed in the United States of America.

Cover based on image from ©iStockPhotos.com/Pamela Moore

ISBN: 978-1-4269-7395-6 (sc)
ISBN: 978-1-4269-7396-3 (hc)
ISBN: 978-1-4269-7567-7 (e)

Library of Congress Control Number: 2011912826

Trafford rev. 10/10/2011

 www.trafford.com

North America & international
toll-free: 1 888 232 4444 (USA & Canada)
phone: 250 383 6864 ✦ fax: 812 355 4082

Dedication – to my friends, family, and loved ones that have joined me for many memorable and enjoyable timeshare vacations and especially Alex for consistently encouraging me.

Preface

Some of life's best moments are associated with receiving keys. A father hesitates as he tosses the car keys to his teenager for their first solo. A car dealer dangles the keys to a bright red sports car as he gives them to the grinning new owner. A desk clerk slides a hotel suite key card across a cold marble counter to young honeymooners. An excited couple receives the keys to their first home from a closing agent. Keys represent accomplishment, control, ownership, access, and anticipation. Receiving the keys to a timeshare unit can provide you with a satisfying feeling as you begin a memorable vacation.

Buying, using, exchanging, renting, and disposing of timeshares is often complicated. But if you educate yourself, you'll be prepared to make wise decisions. Buying a timeshare is a major purchase and a long term commitment. The key to maximizing the value of your ownership is knowledge. Once you own a timeshare, you'll enjoy planning and anticipating regular vacations in a cost-effective way.

You may be considering purchasing a timeshare – or you may already own one or more. This book offers suggestions learned from others and gained by personal experiences. The recommendations are intended to help you get the most out of timeshare ownership by effectively managing the ownership process. For supporting materials and links, visit this book's companion website at:

http://usedtimesharesbook.com

About the Author

Lee enjoys timeshare vacations as diversions from his career as a software engineer. He began by renting timeshare units as an alternative to staying at hotels. He eventually purchased several timeshare weeks and has experience buying them, using them, exchanging them, renting them out, and disposing of them. Along the way, he's researched the timeshare industry and learned many lessons the hard way. His frustration with misconceptions and myths about timesharing, and his desire to help others, has led him to share his advice for cost-effectively obtaining and enjoying timeshares.

Disclaimers

Lee is neither an attorney nor a CPA. Therefore, none of the information in this book should be considered legal or financial advice. The contents are intended to educate and to provide useful suggestions. Please obtain independent professional advice from a licensed and knowledgeable expert regarding your specific legal, financial, and tax-related decisions.

The author does not warrant the correctness of the book's content and makes no claims as to the suitability of the recommendations. The content is exclusively the personal opinion of the author and does not represent the opinions of his employer. Lee provides references to other information sources but makes no representation regarding the content of those sources. He has no control over their content and does not guarantee the reliability or accuracy of other sources of information. If you do not want to be bound by these restrictions, please return this book.

Semantics

The term "timeshare" is used in this book to describe a variety of vacation ownership models including fee-simple deeded ownerships and right-to-use memberships. "Resort" may refer to physical buildings or decision-making organizations that control or manage a timeshare property or plan. The term "week" is used in this book to represent the allocated use time obtained through timeshare ownership, rental agreements, and exchanges which might be less than seven days in some situations. The term "week" also refers to a timeshare ownership interest such as a deeded week or a points contract. In this book, the term "unit" represents the assigned accommodations during the week. A points-based management company refers to the organization that manages the points system and may also refer to the company contracted by the owning entity or the owning entity itself.

Specific timeshare-related companies may not be referenced in this text, but may be identified on the companion website. This book is primarily focused on timeshares located in North America. Although generalizations are made, there are few absolutes and there are almost always exceptions in the diverse timeshare industry.

Table of Contents

List of Figures and Tables

Imagine someone handing you the keys to a resort condominium suite at a beautiful resort and saying "Welcome home!" Feelings of anticipation wash over you as you drag your luggage to your familiar, comfortable retreat. Timeshares can provide pride of ownership and the enjoyment of accessing high quality resort accommodations. Owning a timeshare can also lead to a lifetime of memories. Knowing how to cost-effectively purchase, use, exchange, rent, and dispose of your timeshare can make your vacation experience even better.

Why Learn About Timeshares?

You may have been introduced to the timeshare concept by taking a tempting tour in return for theme park tickets or other incentives. Someone you know may be a timeshare owner who made you feel that you were missing out on a travel secret that they had discovered. However, many of us have heard horror stories of people paying too much for an unused timeshare that subsequently couldn't be traded or sold. While the idea of owning one yourself may be appealing, make sure that you understand what you're getting yourself into before you purchase. Understanding how timeshares work will vastly improve your experience.

"Educated and Informed Owners = Happy Owners"

--Ed Hastry, Founder,
National Timeshare Owners Association (NTOA)

Learning the Truth about Timeshares

There are many myths and misunderstandings about timesharing. The most important thing to do if you're thinking about buying a timeshare is to educate yourself with the facts. This book presents tips and lessons learned to help educate you and enable you to make wise decisions. However, it is not intended to provide legal or tax advice. You should obtain professional help for those issues.

The Web provides a great deal of information about timeshares. However, it is often difficult to discover useful unbiased information. This book's companion website (http://www.usedtimesharesbook.com) provides links to current information. By accessing the book's website, you can click on recommended links rather than having to type in long Web addresses. The website helps you avoid biased information suggested by search engines.

Timeshare Concept

Timesharing is a complex and often misunderstood concept. That's one reason that timeshare sales presentations take so long. Sales people must educate potential buyers and try to overcome their misconceptions. If you understand how timeshares and the timeshare industry work, you can make informed decisions that will save you money and improve your experience. You need to know the facts, not the myths shared by friends or the unfulfilled promises and exaggerations made by some sales people.

Sharing Resort Accommodations

The word "timeshare" conjures up negative images for many people. However, timesharing simply involves people sharing real estate instead of buying it for their sole use. Your mother taught you that sharing is a good thing, right? For many of us, it's intuitive that sharing a resort property that we may only use one week a year makes more sense than buying a vacation home that would sit empty for long periods of time.

Many of us would like to have our own condo on the beach or at a ski resort, but could never afford to buy, furnish, and maintain it. Realistically, unless you're retired, you may only have a few weeks a year to use a vacation home. One reason timesharing is so popular is that it appeals to people with limited time and money who want to enjoy quality lodging at exciting destinations.

In its simplest form, each timeshare owner effectively buys a fraction (share) of a fully furnished condominium unit to use one week per year. Buyers pay for their portion and then pay their share of the resort's ongoing operating and maintenance expenses. Imagine that instead of buying a vacation home, you and 51 strangers agree to buy, maintain, and share a furnished condo at an attractive location. Each owner takes turns using the condo one week per year. Owning a timeshare is also similar to being a part owner of a residential condo complex where owners share the costs of common areas and building exteriors.

Timeshares described in this book involve the shared use of resort properties through deeded ownership or some other type of Right to Use (RTU) privilege for a short period (usually one week) on a regular basis (usually once each year).

Divided Interests

Splitting ownership into 52 weeks is the most common way to divide ownership. For example, a developer might build a resort and sell 50 or 51 weeks to charter owners and retain a week or two to provide time for maintenance. Owners typically use their ownership once a year for a week. However, there are many variations on that theme that are described later. By guaranteeing nearly 100% occupancy (assuming all weeks have been sold), efficiencies result that may provide a lower cost per night than an equivalent hotel situation. The high occupancy level is a key economic aspect of the timeshare business model.

In most situations, buyers receive a deed that they own in perpetuity. However, some timeshares involve paying for the right-to-use one or more resorts for a defined number of years. The specific ownership details are governed by documents that specify the rights and responsibilities of the developer, managers, and owners.

The timesharing concept has been extended to airplanes, boats, motor homes, and campgrounds. However, this book focuses solely on condominium-style resort lodging. Most timeshare accommodations are comparable to furnished private condos that range in size from hotel-style rooms up to spacious suites with three or more bedrooms. They usually have full kitchens, a sitting and dining area, two bedrooms, two bathrooms, and in some cases even laundry rooms.

Timeshare Lifecycle

Real estate developers build timeshare properties to generate profits. They create the resort, sell weeks to initial (charter) buyers, and then move on to other projects. Timeshare projects typically go through similar stages (shown in Figure 1). First, a developer buys land, builds the resort, and furnishes the units. They are betting that a timeshare project will provide a higher profit per unit than other potential uses for the property such as a residential condo or hotel. The developer is motivated to build and sell the new units to initial owners for as high a price as possible. Until the 2008 economic downturn, many timeshare developers were rapidly building more units every year.

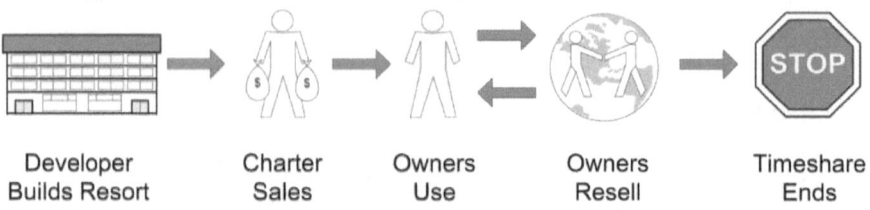

| Developer | Charter | Owners | Owners | Timeshare |
| Builds Resort | Sales | Use | Resell | Ends |

Figure 1. Timeshare Lifecycle

The developer or their affiliated sales company performs legal actions, including establishing codes, covenants, and restrictions (sometimes called program documents) and submits a timeshare plan with the state where the resort is located. They divide ownership into weekly intervals for sale and then place all the units into an inventory pool for retail sales to the initial (charter) owners. As these retail weeks are sold to charter owners, the new owners begin to use the resort. At some point, a Homeowner Association (HOA) usually takes over responsibility from the developer for managing and maintaining the resort. Charter owners may resell their weeks to new owners or pass their ownership on to their heirs.

Eventually, the timeshare arrangement at a particular resort may end. The timeshare plan may have an expiration date. However, the documents may specify that the arrangement will automatically renew for an additional period of years unless a certain percentage of owners vote to terminate the plan. For example, the covenants may specify that the timeshare plan will end in 30 years and be automatically renewed for 10 year periods unless 75% of the owners agree to terminate the plan. Alternatively, the documents may require the owners to vote on whether to continue the plan at the end of the term. With most deeded timeshares, if the plan ends, the owners could sell the property and distribute the proceeds.

The covenants might also allow for the termination before then expiration date under certain circumstances. However, it is highly unlikely that a high percentage of owners would organize and agree to proactively end a timeshare plan.

Timeshare History

Timeshares first appeared over 50 years ago and have evolved in response to buyers' desires. Resort timeshares began in Europe in the 1960s and quickly became popular in the U.S. Many of the first timeshare resorts were created by converting existing motels and apartment complexes. However, most new timeshare resorts are purpose-built complexes developed and sold by large hospitality companies.

Timeshare developers employ a variety of marketing approaches to attract potential buyers to tours and sales presentations. Like many adolescents, the timeshare industry went through a misbehavior stage that led to a bad reputation. Sales incentive giveaways and premiums were often misrepresented. Overly aggressive marketing and sales practices contributed to a poor image of timesharing. This perspective has even been parodied in TV comedy shows that have poked fun at timeshare sales practices and unwise purchasers.

In response to these abuses, the state of Florida banned certain timeshare sales incentives such as sweepstakes in 1983. Securities laws now restrict timeshares from being represented as investments. Many states in the U.S. have now passed consumer protection laws regulating timeshares or have modified existing real estate laws to protect consumers. These laws affect a developer's advertising and disclosures and a buyer's right to cancel a purchase immediately following the sale. However, even in a more regulated and honest marketplace, it is still important that you educate yourself and understand what you're buying.

Mature Timeshare Industry

The timeshare industry has matured, reputable developers have emerged, and government regulation has led to a healthier industry. The current timeshare industry now includes a robust group of high quality development companies, vacation clubs, and resorts.

There are many varieties of timeshares, even resorts that cater to alternative lifestyles and nudists. Most timeshares are near beaches, ski slopes, or theme parks. However, urban timeshares are located in some large cities including New York, San Francisco, Boston, and New Orleans. Location is a key attribute of all types of real estate, including timeshares, because of its effect on supply and demand.

A variety of metrics provide evidence of the time timeshare industry's maturity. The American Resort Development Association (ARDA) is an industry trade group that carefully tracks timeshare industry trends and statistics. They report that over $4.5 billion in timeshare sales occur each year. Timeshare related businesses were one of the fastest growing segments of the travel industry, growing at a rate of 16%/year from 1999-2008.

North America has the most timeshares, followed by Europe. Within North America, the United States has the most, followed by Mexico and then Canada. Mexico is home to some of the most luxurious and highly rated timeshares in the world. However, the U.S. State Department warns citizens to exercise extreme caution before buying real estate in Mexico. Florida has the most timeshares in the United States. Hawaii has a large concentration of highly popular timeshare resorts. ARDA and others have published estimates of timeshare industry statistics that are summarized in Table 1. Due to the dynamic nature of the timeshare industry, these numbers are constantly changing.

Table 1. Timeshare Industry Statistics

Resorts	Countries with timeshare properties	Over 80
	Timeshare resorts worldwide	Around 5,000
	U.S. resorts	Around 1,500
	European resorts	Around 1,300
Owners	Countries with timeshare owners	Over 175
	Timeshare owners worldwide	Over 4 million
	North American owners	Around 2 million
	European owners	Around 1.5 million

Florida has more timeshares than any other state with approximately 375 timeshare properties in 2011. That represents almost a quarter of all timeshares in the United States. Over half of the state's units are located in the Orlando area. Central Florida's popular theme parks contribute to the number of timeshare units located there. Some of the huge Orlando timeshare complexes service thousands of visitors per week. Figure 2 shows the relative concentration of timeshare resort locations.

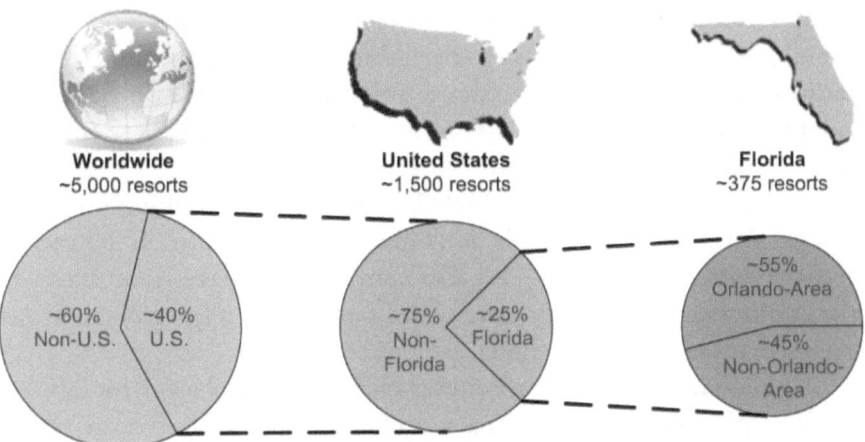

Figure 2. Location of Timeshare Resorts

The timeshare industry has attracted large companies from the entertainment and hospitality industries that own large timeshare components that share their branding. Timeshares operated by these companies, with their recognizable names and well-known reputations, are often associated with consistent quality. Their resorts are often co-located with hotels or theme parks owned by affiliated companies. Mergers and acquisitions continue to alter the landscape of timeshare companies. A current list of large timeshare companies is provided on the companion website.

Timesharing Features

Potential buyers have varying reasons for considering a timeshare purchase. Many people turn to timeshares in search of better vacation experiences than they have received from hotels. Timeshares offer appealing features including unit and resort amenities with varying levels of quality.

Unit Amenities

The room or suite assigned to someone at a timeshare resort is typically called a unit. Most timeshare units are apartment-style suites that are larger than hotel-style bedrooms and most hotel suites. The physical features of a timeshare unit usually include spacious accommodations designed for family-sized groups that are staying several days and more closely resemble a furnished condo than a traditional hotel room. Timeshare units usually have two bedrooms and two bathrooms, but range in size from small hotel room style studios to huge suites with three or more bedrooms.

Timeshare units typically include a kitchen for cooking and food storage. Although some people don't like to cook on vacation, it's nice to have the cost-saving option. It's also convenient to have ready access to snacks purchased at grocery store prices rather than relying on slow and expensive room service at a hotel.

A timeshare unit may be a better choice than a hotel room for families and large groups. With more space, you have room to sleep more people than you'd normally pack into a traditional hotel room. Many hotel chains now have suite options, but these often wind up being slightly larger hotel rooms with efficiency-style kitchens.

Timeshare units provide many of the comforts of home. Most units include a kitchen, dining area, and living area. However, smaller efficiency units are similar to well-equipped hotel rooms. Separate sleeping, sitting, and dining areas increase privacy and enable more activities. For example, one person can sleep in a bedroom while another reads or watches TV in the sitting area.

Some units, called lock-offs, have areas with separate keyed outside entrances and lockable internal doors that allow multiple groups to privately share the same large unit. For example, a two bedroom, two bath unit might be separable into a subunit containing a master bedroom, living room, and kitchen and a second separate subunit that resembles a hotel room. The smaller subunit normally serves as the second bedroom and bathroom of the consolidated unit.

This configuration provides flexibility for sharing and exchanging. However, the subunits can't be resold separately. Lock-off timeshare units are treated as one unit for maintenance fee assessments. The letters "A" and "B" are often used to refer to the subunits (see Figure 3). You may be able to stay two weeks at your resort by using the "A" side one week and the "B" side another. The resort may charge a small lock-off fee to use or exchange the subunits separately.

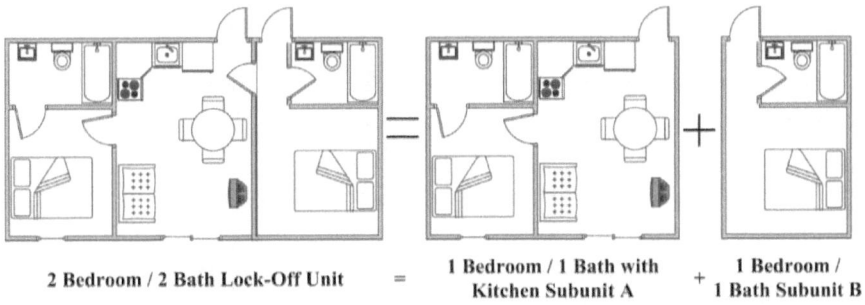

| 2 Bedroom / 2 Bath Lock-Off Unit | = | 1 Bedroom / 1 Bath with Kitchen Subunit A | + | 1 Bedroom / 1 Bath Subunit B |

Figure 3. Lock-Off Unit Configuration

Some units have a washer and dryer. In addition to multiple televisions, many timeshares have DVD players. Free wireless Internet connectivity is now a common feature. Pull-out sofas are often used to help maximize sleeping capacity. The unit should have enough dishes, silverware, linens, and towels for the maximum allowed number of guests.

A key characteristic of a unit is its maximum occupancy limit. Just as most hotels limit how many people can stay there, most resorts limit the number of people who can use a particular timeshare unit. The configuration of a unit affects the comfort level of sharing – mostly due to sleeping, seating, and bathroom access. Exchange companies sometimes refer to private occupancy levels associated with accessing bathrooms, without having to walk through sleeping areas.

Occupancy limits may be required to meet fire codes. However, they also help prevent resorts from becoming overcrowded and keep individual units from suffering too quickly from wear and tear. Overuse leads to higher maintenance costs that are paid by owners. Occupancy restrictions also provide a convenient excuse for limiting the friends and family that want to join you!

Parking availability also limits occupancy levels. Some complexes only have enough parking for one car per unit. Resorts often restrict parking by issuing parking passes upon check-in. Parking passes also limit the use of resort parking lots to those that have legitimate rights to use them.

Resort Amenities

Most timeshare resorts resemble hotels and are located in highly desirable locations that are convenient to shopping and attractions. Quality timeshare resort properties offer amenities similar to high-end hotels including facilities, services, activities, and location-based features.

Timeshare resort amenities vary greatly, but typically include high quality recreation facilities, shops, eating options, and services. Recreation facilities may include pools, hot tubs, fitness rooms, and sports venues with equipment. Many resorts boast tennis courts, shuffle board courts, basketball courts, and game rooms. A few even have their own golf course. Some features are associated with the timeshare's location. These include boardwalks to the beach, theme park shuttles, ski lift access, and hiking.

Timeshares resorts often provide a full schedule of activities for children and adults. Common adult activities include those similar to what you would expect on a cruise ship such as bingo, aerobics, and welcome parties.

Available services may include front desk agents, a concierge, shuttle buses to nearby attractions, on-site DVD rentals, wireless Internet access, and business centers. Excellent customer service significantly improves your enjoyment of your week. Unlike most hotels, smaller timeshare resorts may not staff the front desk all night. Like many hotels, timeshare staff members often provide useful recommendations on dining and entertainment options. However, some resorts employ sales people that try to disguise themselves as concierges in order to encourage guests to attend sales presentations or tours.

Some timeshares have restaurants and bars. A popular option at some Mexican timeshares is to offer an all inclusive option where all meals are served in the resort's restaurants for an additional fee. Timeshares usually have fewer restaurants and bars than hotels of similar size because the guests have their own kitchens and are usually staying for longer periods of time. Shopping may be available at the resort in the form of convenience stores and specialty shops.

Timeshare Quality Tiers

Timeshare properties vary widely in quality and perceptions of quality can be highly subjective. Newer or refurbished resorts have granite countertops and HDTVs while an older property might still retain its original appliances and electronics. Timeshare resorts generally fall into three tiers of quality: high end, mid-level, and low-end.

High end timeshares are located in popular locations. Exchange companies indicate high quality properties with special designations. RCI uses "Gold Crown" to identify top tier resorts and "Silver Crown" to denote the next highest quality. Interval International (II) replaced its often confusing "Five Star" designation with "Premier" (best) and "Select" (second best) designations. Most hospitality companies and entertainment companies that offer timeshares boast high quality resorts that typically receive outstanding reviews from people who have stayed in them. Unfortunately, they typically cost much more than average timeshares and it's much harder to find high end resale weeks for bargain prices. High end units may cost a few thousand dollars to purchase on the resale market or tens of thousands from the developer.

You may be interested in a mid-level timeshare because it's local, or located at your favorite destination. Although these properties are generally older with fewer amenities than the high end timeshares, there are many bargains in this category with resale weeks available for a few hundred dollars.

At the low end of the spectrum are older properties and poorly constructed hotel conversions. Often, owners can't even give these timeshares away or sell them for a $1 bid on the online auction site eBay. Older properties can have major maintenance issues which result in repair costs that must be paid by owners through extra charges called special assessments.

It's impossible to provide recommendations that apply to everyone's situation. However, Table 2 generalizes the advice for people that either already own a timeshare or are considering purchasing one.

Table 2. What to Do if You Own or Want to Own a Timeshare

	Already Own?	**Want to Buy?**
High End	Use and enjoy (see Chapter 3)	Buy resale if possible (see Chapter 2)
Mid-Level	Use (see Chapter 3) or exchange (see Chapter 4) or rent (see Chapter 5)	Buy resale to use for particular reasons (see Chapter 2)
Low End	Upgrade: dispose of your unit (see Chapter 6) and buy a better one resale (see Chapter 2)	Avoid: don't buy and don't accept for free

Timeshare Issues and Challenges

Timeshare owners enjoy the unit and resort amenities at their timeshare resorts. However, despite decades of refinement, timeshares continue to suffer from a variety of problems. Understanding these challenges will help you weigh your timeshare decisions. Owning timeshares involves accepting responsibility, expenses, and restrictions on how you vacation.

Commitment

Buying a timeshare requires making a long term commitment. By purchasing a timeshare, you're promising to pay your share of the operation and maintenance costs of the resort jointly with other owners. Misrepresentations at the time of sale, lack of information or education, and unmet expectations sometimes result in disappointment that leads owners to regret their commitment and want out. However, it can sometimes be difficult to escape ownership responsibilities. A purchased timeshare is not like a service that you can merely call and cancel.

Ownership Expenses

Many popular financial advisors warn consumers to run away from timeshares because of the expense and commitment. Buyers often focus on the initial purchase price of a timeshare. However, timeshare ownership costs also include recurring use-related expenses, and disposal costs.

Consider the total costs as you determine whether you can afford to buy a timeshare.

Initial Purchase Costs

Initial purchase costs include the sales price, transaction expenses, financing costs, and opportunity costs. The biggest factor impacting wildly varying prices is whether you buy from the developer or buy resale. While it is tempting to focus on the price, consider other costs, especially recurring expenses, which may represent the majority of total ownership costs for low-priced resale timeshares.

Once you've found a week for sale that you want to buy, you'll have to pay the purchase price. Purchase prices vary greatly and depend largely on whether you buy from a developer or buy resale. One of the biggest problems with timeshares is that many people pay much more for them than they are worth. Sales people often use high pressure tactics, leading some buyers to pay considerably more for developer-sold timeshares than the resale value.

If you have to finance your timeshare purchase, you should reconsider your decision. Unlike real estate mortgages, timeshare finance interest rates are often as high as credit cards. Most timeshare-related loans are structured as consumer loans instead of mortgages. If you do finance the purchase, make sure there are no prepayment penalties so that you can pay it off as quickly as possible or refinance it some other way. Like a car, don't focus on payments – consider the total cost. Obviously, if you don't finance the purchase, you won't have interest expenses.

Transaction-related costs include the time, energy, and money to select a resort, negotiate a price, and close the sale. Shopping for a timeshare is enjoyable for some and painful for others. Searching for a great deal can be fun. However, many people find sales presentations for developer-sold weeks taxing. After you locate a timeshare resort you like, determine whether weeks at that resort are available for sale.

Completing the purchase transaction includes paying closing costs and the resort's transfer fee. As a real estate transaction, you may have to pay for deed preparation and recording the deed with the local government office. Resorts typically charge the new owner a small administration fee to update their records to reflect the transfer of ownership.

If you pay a large initial price for the timeshare, you're locking up your money until you dispose of the timeshare. The money you could have made by investing those funds is lost, even in the unlikely event that you eventually sell the timeshare and recoup your original outlay. The lost interest or gains that may have resulted if you had invested the money instead of using it to buy a timeshare is called the opportunity cost. The opportunity cost is negligible on a $1,500 resale purchase but substantial on a $50,000 high end developer-sold unit.

Recurring Use-Related Costs

Although timeshares are often advertised as prepaid vacations, there are also ongoing costs associated with owning and using timeshares. Ownership costs include cash expenses for owning and exchanging, as well as the hidden cost of the week's diminishing value.

Ongoing costs include annual maintenance fees and property taxes. There may be occasional special assessments. Additionally, you may pay annual exchange company membership dues and exchange fees if you exchange your timeshare. Also, consider potential expenses such as special assessments, depreciating value (especially if the resort is not well maintained), and travel costs to access the timeshare.

Annual maintenance fees are a large continuing cost related to your share of maintenance and management expenses. Maintenance fees must be paid even if you don't use your week because the resort must be staffed and maintained regardless of whether you do or don't stay there. Annual property taxes are usually billed along with the annual maintenance fees. Special assessments are occasional expenses which occur when unexpected costs arise that must be covered. The HOA may impose any number of special assessments to cover unusual circumstances that take place.

Exchange costs may include annual exchange club membership and exchange fees if you participate in an assisted exchange. Many owners become members of an affiliated exchange company that charge annual membership fees (around $100). When you perform an exchange, there's an additional exchange fee for performing that transaction. More details on exchange costs are provided in Chapter 4.

If you buy a distant timeshare, there will be travel expenses. Travel costs can add up quickly, especially if you're flying several people to your destination and then renting and fueling a car for a week.

Disposal Costs

Eventually, you may have costs when you want to get rid of your timeshare. Depending on the disposal method, there may be advertising costs or broker fees. Closing costs are traditionally paid by the purchaser. Selling may require a significant amount of time and effort if you want to obtain the highest possible price.

An indirect cost is the decreasing value of your purchase between the time you buy it and the time you dispose of it. Timeshare properties usually go down in value, especially if they are not well maintained. As with any real estate, as the property ages, finishes and furnishings become dated, especially if there are no major renovations performed. The decreasing value could be considered an ongoing expense. However, the cost isn't realized until you eventually dispose of the timeshare. The magnitude of the decrease depends on whether the timeshare was purchased from a developer or as a resale from an owner. Just as a new car immediately loses value when you drive it off the lot, a timeshare's value decreases as soon as it is purchased "new" from a developer.

Total Cost of Ownership

Considering all the costs, under certain circumstances, you're financially better off renting hotel suites or timeshare units instead of purchasing a timeshare. Determining the tipping point between purchasing and renting requires careful calculations that take several assumptions into consideration. The total cost of ownership is summarized in Figure 4 below. Dashed boxes in the figure identify potential or optional costs.

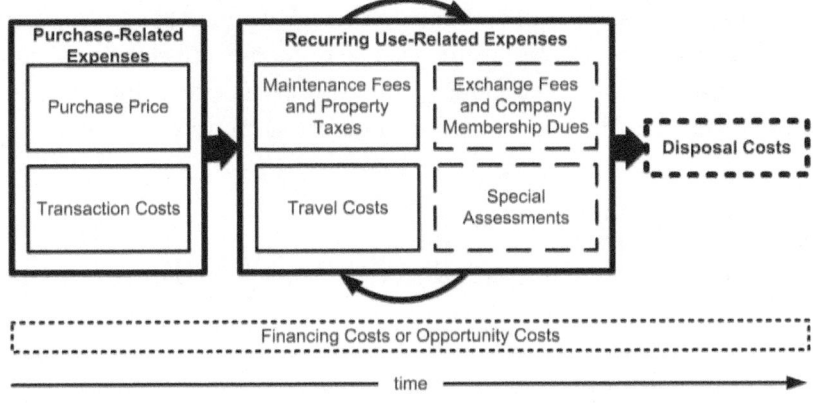

Figure 4. Total Cost of Timeshare Ownership

Restrictions

Timeshare plan rules and regulations create restrictions. Effectively using a timeshare requires discipline to carefully manage reservations (if you don't own a fixed week) and pay maintenance fees on time to avoid interest charges and losing access to your week. Constraints associated with timeshare ownership are related to reserving, using, exchanging, and disposing of the timeshare. If you don't have a fixed week, plan to reserve a scheduled time as there are other owners who also want to access the unit. Non-fixed week owners may discover that there is limited availability when they attempt to reserve choice weeks. They may be required to plan a year in advance to reserve popular weeks. Some people dislike having to use the timeshare in seven day periods. A very common complaint involves a lack of control over escalating maintenance fees and being forced to pay special assessments. Exchangers may be frustrated to find that their unit can't be exchanged for higher end resorts that they're interested in, or that there's little inventory at the destinations they desire for the week they want. When these frustrations elevate to the point that owners want out, they may find that it is very difficult to escape their commitment.

Access Management Approaches

Timeshare buyers purchase the right to occupy a unit for a period of time. Most timeshares are sold and used on a weekly basis. Unlike a hotel, where you pay for the number of nights you want to use, with timeshares you pay for access to a number of days (usually seven) that are accessed each year. Some management companies allow you to split your week into a four day period at one point in the year and a three day period at another, rather than requiring you to access your seven days consecutively. In addition to traditional fixed access periods, some timeshares use point systems to manage access to a variable number of nights or at multiple locations.

Fixed Access Periods

Historically, timeshares were divided into weeks and owners used the same unit the same week each year. However, as the timeshare concept evolved, other options became available. The most common fixed access approaches are described below.

Fixed Weeks

Most of the first timeshares used fixed week systems. Fixed weeks are associated with the same particular week number in a timeshare calendar each year. For example, the owner of week 1 may have access to a Saturday to Saturday timeshare beginning on the first Saturday of the year. Fixed weeks are often paired with a particular at a resort during that fixed week. This approach provides owners with a simple, dependable system. Fixed week owners know exactly when they'll be using their unit and which unit they will occupy.

This approach continues to have value to some people who prefer a particular season and want guaranteed access to their favorite unit. Their week number affects the value of their ownership due to the relative desirability of the week and the specific unit.

Floating Weeks

Although fixed weeks provide dependability and consistency, many owners prefer more flexibility. Developers began to offer floating time which allows owners to select from a set of weeks. The choice of weeks to reserve each year might be unrestricted (weeks numbered 1-52) or might be associated with season designations such as winter or summer at a beach location or snow or mud season at a ski resort.

This approach requires allocating weeks to owners through a reservation system. Since owners are competing for the best weeks within their available pool, resorts have rules and formulas to determine who receives their first choice. The most common method for assigning reservations is first come first served. If you don't plan early and reserve soon enough, you may be relegated to a week that's low on your wish list. Even through your deed may specify a week and unit number, that information may only be used to identify the float period and the unit type.

Some fixed weeks are more prized than others because they're associated with holidays or particular seasons such as snow weather at ski resorts or spring break at the beach. Floating weeks may also be associated with seasons. For example, a summer floating week owner at a particular resort may have their choice of weeks from May through September.

Exchange companies and developers sometimes use color coding to designate high demand weeks as red weeks and less desirable weeks as yellow, green, white, or blue weeks. However, these color designations suffer from inconsistent interpretations and are beginning to fade from use.

Some resorts allow owners to split their seven days of use into two groups of days. For example, owners might use a three day visit during one part of the year, and a four day visit during another part of the year. This option provides owners with flexibility and multiple short getaways and is particularly popular with timeshares located in urban areas. There may be a small fee for splitting the week.

Almost all timeshares are accessed annually. However, some timeshares, called biennials, are accessed every other year. Similarly, some timeshares, called triennials, are accessed every third year. Some buyers couldn't afford annual timeshares or didn't want to timeshare every year, so the industry began offering biennial and triennial weeks. Developers often sell biennial weeks for more than half the cost of annual weeks, in part because of the additional administration overhead costs. Throughout this book, references to annual characteristics should be interpreted as every other year by biennial owners and every third year by triennial owners.

Variable Access Periods Using Points

Points systems provide another approach for controlling access. Some companies sell points-based memberships which enable owners to spend an annual allocation of points to access lodging or purchase other travel-related services. Timeshare points are often referred to as a form of currency that is used to assign accommodations to owners. Many points systems with multiple resort properties are called vacation clubs. Points system ownerships are managed less like real estate than traditional timeshares. The points system concept was introduced in Europe in the 1960s and the U.S. in the 1970s, but didn't become popular until the early 1990s.

The purpose of point systems is to provide more flexibility than traditional timeshare options. Points give owners more control over their vacation experience by allowing them to select a location and duration. For example, one year you might choose a high demand weekend and compromise on unit size by accessing a one bedroom unit that requires fewer points than a two bedroom unit.

Obtaining and Using Points

Some resorts offer owners the option of converting from their traditional deeded timeshare to a points-based system. The associated week is used to determine the number of allocated points that the owners receive each year. Some points systems, sometimes referred to as pure points systems, allow you to buy as many points as you want after a certain minimum point level is purchased. Some systems allow you to buy resale points from other points owners. Even though you're buying into a points-based club, you may still have an identified home resort that serves as the basis for calculating your share of ongoing costs, length of membership, and reservation window. The number of points that you receive for a week associated with a particular resort may be determined in a similar demand-related method as the use of points.

For example, RCI, the largest timeshare exchange company, created a points system in 2000 called RCI Points. For a fee, owners at participating resorts may choose to trade in their traditional timeshare ownership for a set number of points. Owners can usually purchase additional points. The points can then be used each year at many of the resorts that participate in RCI's exchange program. RCI Points members also receive membership in RCI's exchange program – called RCI Weeks. The number of points received each year is allocated based on the number of points purchased or the value of the week converted.

Points can be used to purchase resort stays and other travel services. Some points systems allow owners to use their points only at their home resort but most offer access to multiple properties. Members may have opportunities to use their points for non-timeshare travel options such as car rentals, air travel, cruises, and hotel nights. However, conversion to airline tickets may require several months of advanced notice and additional fees. Some systems even allow you to use your points to pay your maintenance fees.

The number of points an owner needs to use the resort they desire is based on demand factors. For example, an owner with enough points to use a two bedroom off-season week may be able to stay in a one bedroom unit over a long holiday weekend instead. Demand-related factors that affect the number of points required include location, resort popularity, unit size, length of stay, days of week used, and season.

Advantages of Points

The primary advantage of points-based systems is gaining flexibility over where, how, and when you vacation. Another advantage to points systems is that they provide more transparency in exchange value than typical week for week exchange programs. By allocating points for your converted week or buying a certain number of points, you know the exact exchange value you have available. Some programs allow points owners the option of banking or rolling over their points for use the following year. In some cases, you can borrow points from future years for use during the current year. This action is referred to as accelerating your points.

Points provide many options. For example, you might use points to access two weeks in a studio unit rather than a two bedroom unit for a one week period. You can save points for future use by traveling less often, traveling off-peak, staying in smaller units, or staying less than a week at a time.

Disadvantages of Points

Cost is the primary disadvantage of buying or converting into points. It may cost thousands of dollars to convert from a fixed access period to a variable points-based system. Another potential downside of using a points system lies in the potential devaluation that can occur after conversion. The managing company that controls the points system may reduce the value of your points by increasing the number of points needed to access accommodations without increasing the number of points you have available to spend. This could force you to purchase more points to continue accessing the same units at the same time of year. As part of your purchase research, you should try to determine whether the controlling company has a reputation of inflating the number of required points by a large amount each year.

Ownership Types

The term "timeshare" is often used interchangeably with "vacation ownership". But what does it mean to own a vacation? The manner in which a seller conveys access rights to accommodations to a buyer is closely linked with the ownership type. As the timeshare industry evolved, new legal models emerged to support the concept.

The developer or managing company determines the type of ownerships that they sell to charter owners. Therefore, you usually don't have any choice in the type of ownership for a particular resort or system that you have selected. However, it's important to understand the legal implications of your timeshare purchase. Some timeshare interests are deeded like real estate, some timeshares are on leased land, and some are based on right to use memberships. Each ownership type has its own advantages and disadvantages. The most common models are deeded fee-simple ownership and right to use, but other variations exist.

Fee-Simple Deeded Ownership

Most timeshares are legally structured as fee-simple deeded ownerships. Owning this type of timeshare means that you have a fractional ownership in a unit and have a fee title to an undivided interest in common areas. Deeded (fee-simple) owners collectively own the resort. Owners have a real estate deed that is recorded like other real estate with the local government. They hold title to their portion of the resort. They also have the power to collectively make changes to their resort.

Leasehold, a variant of deeded ownership, occurs in places where real estate cannot be traditionally deeded. In a leasehold situation, the lessee has ownership-type rights for a certain number of years. Many of Hawaii's timeshares use this form of ownership because of local customs restricting real estate ownership.

Deeded ownership is advantageous because it provides strong real estate rights, including more control as an owner. Deeds offer ownership security and traditional real estate rights such as the ability to sell, assign, rent, and bequeath. The right to sell is what creates the resale market. Disadvantages with deeded ownership include the expense of foreclosure, complexity of probate, and potentially unlimited liability. Foreclosure on deeded real estate can be expensive for the HOA because the process is often similar to foreclosing on other types of real estate. However, some states are enacting laws to simplify uncontested timeshare foreclosures. Deeded ownership may have to be probated in both the state where the resort is located and the state where the deceased owner lived. A rarely encountered disadvantage involves the unlimited liability for injury and damage shared by owners after insurance settlements are paid.

Deeded timeshares are usually governed by a HOA's board of directors (BoD) elected by the owners. The board typically hires a management company to operate and maintain the resort. The BoD or developer sets an annual budget that results in maintenance fees and approves special assessments.

Although deeded in perpetuity, the associated timeshare program documents may include a termination date. At the termination date, the owners all become tenants-in-common of the overall resort, and must vote on whether to sell the resort and receive their share of the proceeds or continue as a timeshare for another period of time. Alternatively, the plan may automatically renew at the termination date unless blocked by a certain number of owners.

Right to Use Memberships

It's possible to own a vacation interest without a deed. Many newer timeshares are structured as Right to Use (RTU) memberships in which people purchase a lease or contract to access a unit for a set number of years. Some RTU memberships are referred to as leasehold interests or vacation clubs.

Contracted RTU memberships are like long term leases (or licenses) for access to resort accommodations. RTU memberships can be associated with multiple resorts in vacation club points systems or with specific properties. Because some countries restrict foreign ownership of real estate, some resorts sell RTU memberships to provide long term access. If you purchase a right to use timeshare, you usually obtain usage rights for a certain number of years (term).

Right to use concepts have been compared to country clubs that provide access to amenities based on an initiation fee followed by annual dues. Right to use memberships often include additional benefits such as discounts on restaurants and theme park passes. Key terms and conditions include the number of years remaining on the contract.

RTU Membership Varieties

The value of your membership will likely decrease as time goes on and fewer years of access are left on the lease. Your access rights and obligation terminate at the end of the membership. Your contract should stipulate whether you can transfer the remaining years through donation, sale, or inheritance.

There are different types of RTU timeshare membership programs. Individual timeshare resorts are sometimes set up as RTU properties, but this approach is more common with vacation clubs. Many vacation clubs are structured as multi-site RTU systems with resorts in multiple locations to provide members with options much like an internal exchange system. Points systems are commonly used for allocating access to vacation club resort properties.

Home Resort Tie-In

Vacation clubs may tie membership to a particular home resort and week to calculate maintenance fees and points allocations. RTU owners may receive special benefits at their home resort. For example, owners may be able to reserve a week at their home resort earlier than reserving other resorts.

Pure points systems focus on a set number of points rather than being associated with a home resort. A membership in a pure point system is considered tangible personal property rather than deeded real estate ownership.

RTU Ownership

As a member, you're not a true owner of the resort's real estate. RTU participants buy memberships to access resort properties. The properties are owned by a managing company that is associated with the developer, a vacation club, or a trust that operates for the benefit of its members. RTU members don't own a timeshare as real estate (fee-simple deeded interest), instead they make an agreement with a company to access accommodations. Effectively, they're entering into a form of lease. Some people argue over the semantics of owning or leasing. You're purchasing an interest in a property, but you don't own it. You're often buying an annual allotment of points for a given number of years or in perpetuity.

The terms and conditions of your RTU ownership should be specified in a contract or lease agreement. The document may be recorded with the local government office, but that doesn't mean that it's a deed in the fee-simple title sense. However, it does reassure some purchasers because their purchase is recorded in the public records. The term of the lease is the length of time that you have access to their accommodations.

Unlike fee-simple deeded ownership, in right to use situations, the people who use the resort do not normally own it. Instead, some entity continues to own the resort after the weeks are sold to members. Since members are effectively just leasing resort access, the company that sells the memberships owns the land and buildings. The owning entity might be the developer, a company associated with the developer, a hospitality company, or a trust that represents its members. The resort's owner may outsource membership administration to a separate management company.

The resort's owner sells RTU memberships with temporary lease-type rights and possibly some level of control. Some RTU systems allow member participation or advocacy through elected representation. However, unlike the HOA at a deeded timeshare resort, true control remains in the hands of the owning company which may sell its stake to a new entity. The owning company may be able to unilaterally change some of the rules of the program.

RTU Membership Lifecycle

RTU memberships are marketed and sold similarly to traditional fee-simple deeded timeshares. However, the purchase price (sometimes called an initiation fee) only provides access for a limited number of years. Purchasers enjoy access to one or more resorts and pay annual dues that are similar to traditional maintenance fees.

At the end of the membership period, access rights revert to the resort's owners. A few RTU memberships require the owner of the resort property to share some of the profits with the members at the end of the membership. Some companies have even promised to return an amount equal to or greater than the original purchase price. However, there is an opportunity cost because potential interest on the initial price paid is lost.

RTU Membership Advantages

RTU memberships expire without any continuing responsibility on the member's part, a definite advantage over owning an older timeshare that is difficult to unload. In a few cases, memberships involving trusts may have residual values. RTU memberships often incorporate built-in multi-resort access which provides more scheduling flexibility. Many RTU memberships are offered by established hospitality companies with excellent reputations for maintaining the quality of their properties. The RTU membership involves less liability than a traditional, fee-simple timeshare. Furthermore, some RTU memberships supply access to non-timeshare travel services. However, many of these services may be available from other sources at a lower cost. RTU ownerships may be the only option in some foreign countries whose ownership laws complicate real estate ownership.

RTU Membership Disadvantages

RTU membership owners typically have limited control over their resorts and the terms of their memberships, an issue that owners of fee-simple deeded timeshares do not share. Since membership owners typically don't select the property manager, you may be stuck with a poorly performing property manager selected by the owning company. Normally, RTU memberships are worthless at the end of their term because the right to access the resort has expired. RTU memberships may be tied to points that are devalued as the number of points required to stay at particular resorts is increased. Additionally, it may be difficult or impossible to use an outside (unaffiliated) exchange company with an RTU membership. Since you typically don't have real estate ownership rights, you may lose the value of your membership if the controlling entity goes out of business. At that point, you may become just another creditor trying to get a share of the company's assets.

RTU Membership Summary

RTU membership systems represent a more complex approach to timesharing. However, they provide some significant advantages over traditional deeded timeshare ownership. The key to successful use of an RTU membership is to understand how many points you're purchasing and how many you'll need to access the accommodations you desire. Since RTU memberships are basically a lease, be sure you understand the terms. Make certain you understand the rules regarding reserving, renting, exchanging, and calculating fees.

Other Ownership Models

A few timeshares operate as neither fee-simple deeded timeshares nor as right to use timeshares. One attractive alternative is a system in which buyers receive a permanent equity ownership position in a company that owns and manages resorts. These non-deeded equity systems limit liability because owners are more like stockholders in a corporation than owners of real estate property. The owning company is a permanent legal entity owned by voting members. These types of organizations provide owners with equity in the entity, voting rights, and liability protection. Figure 5 compares and contrasts the most popular models with the non-deeded equity systems.

	Fee-Simple Deeded	Right to Use	Non-Deeded Equity
Equity Ownership	✓		✓
Permanent	✓	✓ (some)	✓
Limited Liability		✓	✓

Figure 5. Comparing Timeshare Models

Alternatives to Traditional Timesharing

One argument against timesharing is that several other viable options exist for obtaining reasonably priced high quality resort accommodations. Alternatives to traditional timesharing include renting a hotel room, renting a timeshare, and buying a fractional ownership or destination club.

Hotels provide a wide variety of choices and require no commitment. However, high quality hotels are expensive. With a hotel, you're not restricted to a time of year or number of days. Extra resort amenities, such as room service and daily maid service, are available at a hotel while these are not typically found at a timeshare.

You don't have to buy a timeshare to access timeshare resort accommodations. If you decide not to commit to timesharing by becoming an owner, you may be able to rent a timeshare unit. Owners who aren't using their units, and resorts with unsold or foreclosed units, rent them out. Renting a timeshare unit also provides an excellent introduction to timesharing for those that are considering buying.

Many factors and assumptions impact a comparison of vacationing options over the long term. One of the biggest arguments used by timeshare salesmen is that it's cheaper than renting hotel rooms over the long run, assuming you'd only be vacationing one week per year. This opinion relies on several assumptions. Table 3 identifies typical costs in 2011 associated with a timeshare purchase compared to other vacation options. Other than the initial cost of a timeshare purchase, these figures will likely grow annually at the rate of inflation over the time period of use. The nightly use figures for purchased timeshares assume 30 years of use and no residual value. These figures are provided for illustrative purposes and are not tied to averages from any scientific studies.

Table 3. Rental and Purchase Option Comparison Illustration

	Rent		Buy	
	Resort Hotel Room or Suite	**High Quality Vacation Condo or Timeshare**	**High Quality Timeshare From Developer**	**High Quality Resale Timeshare**
Up-Front / Initial Costs	None	None	$15,000 - $80,000	$500 - $10,000
Typical Annual Cost	$150 - $500 per night	About $1,400 ($700 - $2100)	$500-$1200 maintenance fees	
Additional Expenses	Taxes, resort fees, parking	Taxes	Special assessments (when they apply)	
Typical Use	No maximum nor minimum	One week	One week	
Cost per Night of Use	$180 - $600	About $200 ($100-$330) - $330	$200 - $300	$200 - $300

Fractional ownership is a timeshare concept that divides an annual ownership into fewer than the 52 weekly intervals characteristic of a traditional timeshare. Owners of fractional have several weeks or even months of use. For example, a quarter share gives an owner three months of access each year. However, because the costs are distributed over fewer owners, the costs are greater than only owning a week.

More affluent vacationers may consider another version of timesharing, often called Destination Clubs, involving high end multi-million dollar homes that are accessed for multiple weeks during the year.

Navigating this Book

This book focuses on buying, using, exchanging, renting, and disposing of used timeshares – resale timeshares that have already been sold by the developer. However, whether you buy from a developer or from another owner, you can benefit from this information. This book's organization aligns with the timeshare ownership lifecycle summarized in Figure 6.

Figure 6. Book Roadmap

If you already own through retail or resale purchase or inheritance, you may want to skip Chapter 2 which describes the purchasing process. Chapter 3 provides suggestions for maximizing the use of your unit. Chapter 4 describes methods for successfully exchanging your timeshare. Chapter 5 explains how to rent out your timeshare. Chapter 6 provides suggestions for disposing of a timeshare. Chapter 7 presents some predictions about the possible future of the timeshare industry.

Additional resources are provided in sections at the end including a list of recommended information sources, lists of federal holidays, timeshare calendars, a glossary, and an index. There are also many online sources of information that are easily available through links on the companion website:

http://www.usedtimesharesbook.com

The easiest step in the timeshare ownership cycle is buying. Many people get caught up in the excitement of purchasing a timeshare. Buyers often make spontaneous choices instead of informed decisions. You may be anticipating enjoying your timeshare and making lasting memories with your loved ones for many years to come. However, the buying process should be a business negotiation rather than an emotional decision. Question whether you really want to make the commitment and carefully examine your motivations for making the purchase.

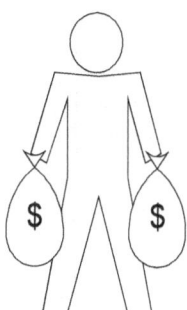

Why Buy a Timeshare?

Before you buy a timeshare, think about what is important to you. Many people buy on impulse after participating in a convincing sales presentation without performing any research. The primary reason for buying a timeshare is to cost-effectively access high quality resorts and their units' amenities. Buy a timeshare for its financial and emotional benefits instead of the wrong reasons.

Financial Benefits

The financial benefit of owning a timeshare ultimately comes down to getting more value for your money than other lodging options. Any financial benefits result from contrasting comparable rental accommodations into the future while considering probable increases from inflation.

If you decide to purchase a resale timeshare, you might enjoy the comfort of a short term rental condo for the price of an average hotel room (see Figure 7). Judging the financial benefits of a timeshare purchase requires making assumptions about your future vacation activities.

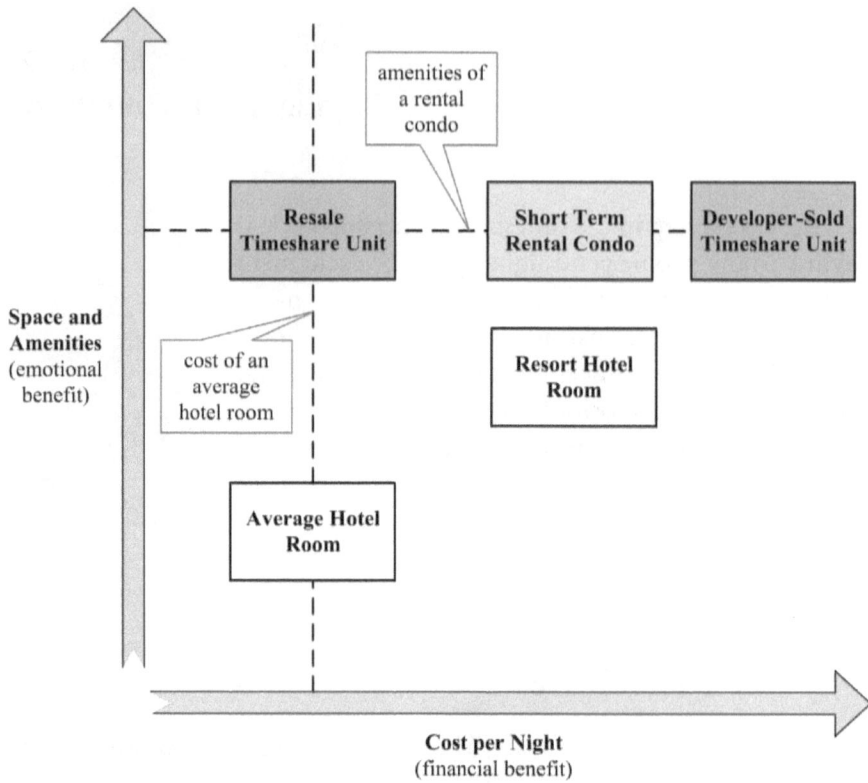

Figure 7. Accessing High End Accommodations at Hotel Costs

Making Assumptions

A fair comparison between a timeshare purchase and other options requires several basic assumptions. A popular motivation for buying a timeshare is to partially control the cost of future vacations. Many salespeople tout the concept of prepaid vacations. However, you should consider a variety of cost factors, including the opportunity cost of the initial purchase and the ongoing annual maintenance fees.

The economic value of a timeshare week is highly dependent on the initial purchase price. Since most existing owners can resell their timeshare, you have the opportunity to buy on the secondary market. You can find resale timeshares at very reasonable prices or even for free. You may be able to eventually resell your timeshare and recoup some of your initial purchase price.

Timeshares offer an alternative to hotel stays. Ultimately, a decision to buy a timeshare comes down to whether it makes financial sense to commit to long term access to timeshare resorts rather than utilizing more traditional options. The closest alternative to timesharing is renting a hotel suite. Several hotel chains now offer suites hotels with multiple rooms and studio size kitchens. However, many of these hotels target long term business travelers and are not often available in resort settings. Compared to renting two rooms or a suite at a resort hotel, timeshares can be much cheaper, especially if bought as a resale. Table 4 contrasts the costs of using a timeshare to those of renting a hotel suite.

Table 4. Contrasting Timeshare Costs to Hotel Rental Costs

Ownership Costs for a Typical Timeshare Week	Rental Costs for a Comparable Hotel Suite
One-time initial purchase price	Recurring nightly rate
Deductible property taxes	Hotel taxes and municipal fees
Maintenance fees that typically escalate annually	Rents that escalate with inflation and market pressures
Special assessments	No responsibility for unanticipated problems
Potential disposal costs	No disposal costs
Potential for a small residual value	No residual value
Dining costs may be lower if kitchen is utilized	Typically requires eating out most meals unless suite has a full kitchen
Potential legal liability	No liability

Spending money on a timeshare is a financial benefit only if you spend less than you would otherwise. Salespeople often talk about locking in costs, and saving on accommodation expenses that will likely escalate over the long term. They may contrast timeshare costs to the uncertainty of future hotel rate increases, which you might reasonably assume will increase at the rate of inflation. This argument, however, doesn't take into account the fact that maintenance fees also typically grow at about the same rate as inflation as the costs of operating and maintaining the resort increase. Hotel rates could increase faster than inflation as hotel companies try and maximize rents, but the lodging market would likely eventually correct any supply/demand imbalances. Some salespeople will also claim that there's a potential for rental income from a timeshare.

However, when rents do materialize, they rarely cover the maintenance fee costs for the year.

Calculating the Benefit

Some owners have developed complex formulas and spreadsheets that account for many factors to compare nightly costs of timeshares to other options. Accurate savings forecasts should consider assumptions regarding your future behavior such as the frequency of use and the impacts of inflation. At first glance, it would appear that the hotel suite is a better choice. However, the average cost per night may be significantly lower for timeshares in the long run if you buy resale and consistently vacation there every year.

Emotional Motivations

Besides the resort and unit amenities described in the previous chapter and the financial benefits enumerated in the prior section, you may enjoy the intangible emotional benefits that come with owning a timeshare. Pride of ownership, forced vacations, predictability, comfort, and the opportunity to share the unit all motivate people to purchase.

Timeshares provide pride of ownership. Some timeshare owners, especially those that bought resale, are proud of the bargain they found and the money they've saved over the years. It's also a good feeling knowing you're an owner and not just a renter.

Timeshare ownership may serve as a forcing factor to encourage vacationing. Knowing you need to use or lose your week may give you the reason you need to get away for a well deserved and needed break. It gives you a good excuse to tell your boss that you have to take some of your vacation time. Required scheduling also encourages procrastinators to plan ahead and take annual vacations.

Timeshares provide predictability with guaranteed access to the same size and consistent quality of accommodations each year. At well-maintained resorts, you may arrive and be pleasantly surprised by upgrades and improved furnishings and decorations.

Timeshares provide a comfortable feeling by returning to a familiar favorite location. Owning a timeshare can feel like having your own condo on the beach or at the slopes. Spacious well-appointed timeshare units provide a home away from home. By returning each year, you get to know the staff, fellow guests, and the local area. You might also feel safer staying at higher end accommodations that attract fellow owners like yourself that are less transient than guests at a hotel. Owning a timeshare is an opportunity to share with friends and family. Some may join you on your vacation while others may use your week when you are unable to do so. A timeshare may also serve as a legacy or an inheritance if that is an important consideration for your family.

Wrong Reasons for Buying

Exaggerated sales presentations may encourage some people to purchase timeshares based partly on incorrect information. Wrong reasons for buying a timeshare include buying primarily to exchange, to invest in real estate, to access exchange company inventory, to leave as an inheritance, or to get a bargain.

Don't buy a unit merely to try exchanging it for better properties. While it is possible, you have very little control and must be patient, flexible, and lucky (see Chapter 4 on Exchanging).

A timeshare purchase is not a financial investment in the sense of buying rental property to lease out. Few people successfully rent their week for a profit. It's hard to find renters yourself, and if you use the resort's services, you only receive a portion of the rental income (see Chapter 5 on renting).

Like a cruise, a timeshare purchase should not be considered an investment in anything other than an enjoyable vacation. A timeshare is basically a partially prepaid vacation. You are purchasing the right to access accommodations in the future, but will have to fulfill your commitment to help maintain and operate the resort. Consider the costs and the potential benefits that you will obtain from using your week. However, be realistic about the fact that you will likely recover little if any of your original outlay of funds.

Don't buy a timeshare just to access an exchange company for gaining access to their perks, such as inexpensive rentals. The weeks they make available to rent are often less desirable weeks such as mud season at ski resorts or hurricane season at beach resorts. Also, you can rent timeshares from other sources besides the exchange companies.

Don't buy a timeshare for the sole purpose of leaving it to your kids – they would probably prefer cash. You may also be burdening them with probating the ownership. If they accept the timeshare, but then realize they don't want it, they'll have to figure out how to dispose of it. If they're unfamiliar with timesharing, that may take them considerable time and effort.

You shouldn't buy a cheap resale timeshare only to resell it. When you see a resale unit available for a fraction of the price an owner paid to the developer, you may be tempted to jump on the bargain. Even though you'd probably save a considerable amount of money compared to buying from a developer, keep in mind that it isn't easy to resell most timeshares. Similarly, don't accept a free timeshare without considering the commitment you're making.

> "Rationalization is the key to mental health."
>
> --Bill Scheessele
> Mastering Business Development, Inc. (MBDi)

Rationalizing Your Decision

Consider all the costs, commitments, and restrictions before choosing to purchase a timeshare. Additionally, anticipate the financial and emotional benefits. After considering all the advantages and disadvantages, you ultimately must decide whether it makes sense for you to buy. If you expect to use the timeshare frequently over the next 10-20 years, the maintenance fees are less than the cost of renting the unit, and the purchase price is low, it may make sense to buy. Statistics indicate that many timeshare owners buy additional weeks, a sure sign that they recognized value in their original purchase.

Purchase Options

Many people associate buying a timeshare with enduring high pressure sales presentations. Many buyers purchase on-site from the developer after visiting the resort, taking a tour, and listening to a sales pitch. However, many purchasers now buy resale timeshares online, sometimes without first visiting the resort. You can buy a timeshare from a developer or buy resale through the resort, a broker, or directly from the current owner.

Buying from a Developer

Newer and expanding resorts sell developer-owned weeks using elaborate marketing campaigns with incentives for touring and participating in sales presentations. If a resort is still actively selling weeks, they will have a sales department. However, their price may be significantly higher than similar weeks available from other sources. Most first-time timeshare purchasers buy retail from a developer. This stems from intensive advertising and incentives that bring buyers into contact with highly trained professional sales people. Developers use giveaways, tours, and free tickets to shows and theme parks to influence potential buyers to participate in sales presentations. These marketing tools contribute to the high cost of developer-sold timeshares.

Sales presentations often include aggressive techniques. Surviving a timeshare sales presentation is the subject of an entire book. Although the experience can be stressful or frustrating, it can also be a useful source of information. If you agree to participate in a sales presentation, stipulate an ending time before committing to the meeting. An average time for a timeshare tour and presentation is about 90 minutes. However, it may last several hours. The salesperson will try to establish a relationship with you and relax you before starting any high pressure sales techniques. Timeshare salespeople naturally focus on the resort or RTU system that they're selling. Therefore, your interests and desires may not align with the resort or timeshare system the salesperson is offering. If you decline their invitation to purchase, you'll likely be handed off to one or more other sales people before you are allowed to leave with your incentive gift.

Don't go to the presentation just for the incentives – go to learn. Verify information provided by the sales people and get all their promises in writing. Remember, you're dealing with a professional who has been trained to counter all your objections. Be honest with the salesperson and practice saying "no". You might want to explain that you're doing research and you're not ready to buy. They may try and change your resolve with offers that supposedly expire that day. Although some timeshare salespeople have a bad reputation, there are many honest, ethical professionals in the industry.

> Homer: "Remember when those smooth-talking guys tried to sell me a time-share vacation condo?"
>
> Marge: "You bought four of them! Thank God the check bounced."
>
> --Simpsons Episode 9.13 "The Joy of Sect"

There are a few advantages to buying from a developer including some benefits that may not be available to resale purchasers. It's easier to buy from a developer because you can easily find them, tour a resort, receive an education about their particular system, and quickly complete the transaction. Tourists in markets such as Orlando are bombarded by advertising on billboards, at hotels, information desks, ticket outlets, and in malls. Many people enjoy receiving the rewards such as show tickets or free hotel stays offered by salespeople in return for their active participation in a sales presentation.

Developers help educate potential buyers about timeshares through their marketing efforts and tours. Buying from the developer also offers an opportunity for human face-to-face interaction with someone who can answer your questions, address your concerns, and encourage you to buy. If you decide to buy from a developer, they often provide a speedy and efficient closing process.

Buying from a developer may be the only way to purchase in new developments, or to buy the most highly desired weeks or units. Hotel-associated timeshare vacation clubs sometimes provide additional features only available to those that purchase from the developer. For example, they may allow vacation club points to be converted to points in the hotel chain's customer loyalty program. In that way, club members may be able to access hotel nights in the same way as a person that frequents the company's hotel chain.

The primary disadvantage to buying from the developer is the marketing overhead cost. When you buy from the developer, a large portion of the sales price covers the developer's investment in sales and marketing. Much of the difference between retail and resale prices can be attributed to this differential. Up to 50% of the price offered by the developer covers the overhead costs including sales presentation incentives, advertising, salespeople, and administrative staff. Therefore, if you purchase from a developer, you shouldn't expect to recoup more than 50% of what you paid when you resell your week. If more people understood timeshares, the developers wouldn't need to spend as much on marketing and might be able to pass those savings along to buyers who wouldn't need to participate in annoying sales pitches.

Some resale advocates disdain the idea of buying from a developer. Nevertheless, developer sales represent a necessary component of the timeshare supply chain. Without charter sales, the developer wouldn't be motivated to create the project and there would be no units available for resale.

> "The biggest secret about timeshares is that developers don't want you to know [that it isn't] necessary to sit through a high-pressure sales presentation in order to purchase a timeshare."
>
> --Lisa Ann Schreier
> author of *Timeshares for Dummies*

Buying Resale

Most timeshare owners have the right to resell their timeshare. This creates a secondary market – like buying a used car from a previous owner instead of a new car from a dealer. However, with timeshares, there's usually no difference between a new (retail) or used (resale) timeshare week. The least expensive source for buying a timeshare is almost always directly from an owner that's trying to resell their week. There are many owners who want to sell their timeshare interest. This creates a large supply of resale units. Existing owners may try to sell on their own, use a broker, or hire someone to help them.

The price you pay for a resale week will be considerably less than the same week from a developer because the existing owners are typically more motivated and don't have high marketing and overhead costs to cover. You may be able to buy a resale timeshare directly from a sales person at the resort, through a broker, or directly from the existing owner.

Purchasing at a resort doesn't necessarily mean you're buying from the developer. The resort where you want to buy may continue to sell weeks even though the original charter weeks have been sold out for some time. On-site brokers at some resorts represent owners who want to sell and foreclosed weeks owned by the HOA. Dealing with the resort's broker helps avoid misunderstandings since they're very familiar with their resort and the different types of ownerships they offer. Some people feel more comfortable dealing with someone they've met at the resort instead of a stranger that posts an online advertisement. An onsite broker may also be able to give you a tour of the unit types available for sale.

A resale owner may be represented by a broker or a resale company. Sellers pay brokers a commission from the sale. Therefore, their asking price may be higher to cover the broker's fee. Licensed timeshare brokers are professionals that understand the resale process. Brokers may maintain their own online list of available weeks or list them on websites managed by others.

Some owners resell their weeks on their own. They may advertise in classified ads or use an eBay auction. It may be difficult in some cases to arrange a tour of the resort when you're buying through a broker or directly from an owner. Unfortunately, an owner may not fully understand the sales process.

If you're thinking about buying a timeshare, consider buying resale before you make your decision. There's a huge difference in costs and the processes between purchasing retail from a developer or buying a resale week from an owner. It's easier, but more expensive, to buy from the developer. Buying a resale week is cheaper but takes more effort.

Choosing a Purchase Option

You have a choice between buying from a developer and buying resale. The easiest way to obtain high demand weeks at high quality resorts is to buy from a developer. However, this is often a very expensive and unnecessary option. There are very few differences between buying resale units and buying from the developer – except for the initial price. The resale purchase process may be longer and more difficult than dealing with the developer's professional sales staff, but it may be worth it to save a great deal of money. Table 5 summarizes purchase options.

Table 5. Comparing Purchase Sources

Source		Advantages	Disadvantages
Developer		• Easy access for tour and resort information • Possible incentives • Easy process	• Expensive • Possibly high pressure sales approach
Resale	**Directly from the Resort**	• Lower cost than developer sold weeks • Very familiar with resort and ownership types	• Available weeks may be less desirable • Hard to find prime location / weeks
	Through a Broker	• Expert on process • Legally regulated • Intermediary eliminates awkwardness of negotiating directly with seller	• Commission costs • Middleman may confuse communication
	Directly from an Existing Owner	• Least expensive purchase price • Dealing directly with seller avoids miscommunications	• May require dealing with a stranger • Owner may not understand their ownership or the process

Purchase Process

Once you've decided to buy a timeshare, analyze your preferences and select a resort that you'd enjoy owning. Then find available weeks for sale and determine a fair price. After you complete these preliminary steps, negotiate the price and close the deal. The following section provides tips on successfully completing the purchase process (summarized in Figure 8).

| Prioritize | Select Resort | Find Units for Sale | Determine Value | Negotiate Price | Complete Purchase |

Figure 8. Timeshare Purchase Process

Prioritizing Your Vacationing Preferences

Before you begin looking for a timeshare, think about how you like to vacation. Prepare by identifying your priorities and calculating your financial and time budgets.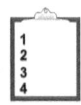

The first step in buying a timeshare is deciding what you want to buy. That means that you need to engage in some self examination in order to determine your vacationing preferences. This shouldn't be an emotional decision made when you're particularly vulnerable to sales pitches, like when you're on your honeymoon.

Potential owners find it useful to list their personal priorities. That list will likely change as you age and your family evolves. Estimate how many years you think you'll use the timeshare. Your children may not want to go with you to theme parks as often when they are in their late teens, but they may bring your grandchildren to join you in 20 years.

How picky are you? Do you like to vacation in style? Is daily maid service important? Do you want to order from room service at 3 o'clock in the morning? What are the most important amenities to you? Know your expectation level. Are high-end amenities important? What about quality finishes like granite countertops? Do you enjoy a large heated pool? Remember that you're taking responsibility for maintaining these luxuries through your annual maintenance fees.

As with any type of real estate, location is key. Think about where you like to visit to enjoy your interests. Do you like hanging out on the beach, visiting theme parks, skiing the slopes, or playing golf each day?

Remember that you're going to be at the timeshare for a full week, so make sure you'll have plenty of options.

Affordability is an important factor in considering your purchase. Don't buy more than you can afford. If you borrow to purchase, use lower-cost financing approaches rather than taking out a consumer loan from a developer with high interest rates.

How often do you vacation? How many weeks of vacation do you get? If your timeshare is located a long distance from your permanent home, then you may be less likely to use it frequently. Think about how you're going to get there so you can factor in transportation costs. Unless you work for an airline or have tons of frequent flier miles, flying may be expensive, especially for several people. That beautiful Hawaiian timeshare resort may be very expensive for a large family to access every year.

The most important factor in selecting a timeshare is its personal value to you. Pick a timeshare you plan to use the majority of time yourself. Just as you would select a cruise that sails to ports of call that interest you, select a timeshare based on its location. In the case of multi-location vacation clubs, consider the multiple potential location options.

Selecting a Resort or Points System

After you've identified what you are looking for, you need to select a particular property. Even if you're interested in a point system, you may have to select a home resort that's used to calculate maintenance fees and special assessments. There are many timeshares available for purchase, so don't buy the first one you see. Decide which one you want, and then figure out how to buy it.

Performing Your Due Diligence

A surprisingly large number of resale purchasers actually buy their week without ever visiting the resort. However, like test driving a car, you should try before you buy by staying there in a rental unit if possible. Keep in mind that you may be treated better if you return as an owner.

If you can't stay overnight, at least visit the property and ask to look around. You may be able to avoid a sales pitch if you're willing to forgo the incentives they normally offer for participating in a sales presentation. Also, if it's an established property that is no longer in active sales, the front desk personnel may allow you to explore the resort and see some of the units. Touring the resort is a key step in the research process. However, eager sellers or resale sales people may tell you that a tour of the resort is unnecessary or that researching the purchase will cause you to miss a fleeting opportunity to grab a bargain.

Learn as much as you can about the resort that you're considering. Ask about upcoming special assessments and the cost of maintenance fees. Find out who manages the resort and whether there's an independent HOA. Also, ask if the resort is affiliated with an exchange company and whether they participate in an internal exchange program.

Discover what other people think of the resort by looking at reviews and ratings on websites and in magazines. Remember that some reviewers are biased or exaggerated. Some owners try to increase perceived value by writing glowing reviews. Other reviewers are disappointed renters or exchangers. You may come across review websites that mainly target the hotel industry, so renters may have left poor reviews over disappointment with the timeshare approach compared to what they're used to with hotels. For example, some reviewers are shocked at the lack of daily housekeeping because they're not familiar with timeshare customs.

Word of mouth advertising is extremely powerful. Developers recognize that and sometimes offer rewards such as discounted maintenance fees to current owners that encourage you to buy. Therefore, your friends may have multiple reasons to suggest that you join them as owners at their resort.

A timeshare presentation does not provide unbiased facts. The salespeople want to sell you their timeshare and focus solely on promoting the benefits and countering all your objections and negative perceptions. Consider contacting the exchange company affiliated with the resort to learn about relative demand for exchanged weeks from the resort. If the resort is affiliated with RCI and you know an RCI Weeks member, they can look up the potential trading power for the resort, timeframe, and unit type that you're considering buying.

Choosing an Access Method and Unit Type

Decide whether to buy a deeded timeshare or to buy into a points system. You may want the flexibility that points systems provide or the consistency of owning at your favorite resort. If you're buying a deeded timeshare, select one that you expect to use most of the time. If you're thinking about buying primarily to trade often in order to access a variety of properties, consider buying into a points-based system instead. If you want to own a deeded timeshare and expect to occasionally perform exchanges using that week, consider its potential exchange value.

Resorts typically offer a variety of unit types that may differ in size, view, and location. Think twice before you buy a small one bedroom, studio, or hotel room size unit because it will be more difficult to exchange and eventually sell. Buying a lock-off unit may provide flexibility for using, renting, and exchanging your week.

Finding Timeshares for Sale

Once you've selected a resort, look for weeks available for sale. If the property is still in active sales by the developer, you first need to decide whether to buy from the developer (referred to as new or retail) or from an owner (referred to  as used or resale). It's easier to find retail weeks for sale, than it is to find resale weeks.

Eventually, charter owners sell their ownership rights to resale buyers either directly or with the help of the resort. Some weeks go back to the developer or to the Homeowner Association (HOA) through a foreclosure process. Therefore, if you're looking for weeks for sale, the primary sources are the developer, the resort, and resale owners.

Initially, developers build resorts and turn them over to sales people who sell weeks to charter buyers. It's easy to find developer weeks for sale because their marketing firms overwhelm potential buyers with advertisements. Developers often disguise advertisements as travel deals or dangle incentives for participation in sales presentations. If you want to initiate contact with a developer's sales people, you can find their contact information on the resort's website.

Begin your hunt for available weeks by contacting the resort. They know the most about their product. Learn about their asking prices and availability. Resorts that are no longer in active sales sometimes have their own resale brokers who represent owners or sell foreclosed weeks. They may also know owners who are considering selling. The resort may allow you to advertise your interest in buying a resale week in their newsletter, on their bulletin board, or on their website.

Timeshare owners and their brokers advertise timeshares for sale on the Web and in print publications. Searching for a great buy can be a fun hobby in itself. Some people are practically addicted to trolling resale websites and online auctions in search of an excellent deal. Sources of leads include multiple timeshare listing websites, timeshare magazines that include classified ads, and auction sites such as eBay. Resale timeshares are advertised everywhere - even on the radio.

Real estate brokers working for timeshare resale companies sometimes sell timeshares for owners. The brokers help sellers connect with buyers. Some operate primarily online, while others have physical locations in areas with large concentrations of timeshares.

Many resale timeshares are sold using online auctions. Online auction site eBay is one of the best sources for bargain timeshares. Auctions often provide the lowest price, but also serve as a dumping ground for low end units, many of which are offered for a starting bid of $1 plus closing costs and transfer fees. Some bidders use sniping software to try and win auctions with a last-minute offer. Be sure to learn about the eBay purchase process before you make your first bid. Also, keep in mind that technically you're not buying, but entering into negotiations (since you can't buy real estate on eBay). BidShares also has as an auction site, but its auctions are long term and have much less activity than eBay, leading it to appear more like a listing service.

As with everything else in our modern lives, the Internet has greatly simplified communications. Purchasers no longer rely on classified ads in obscure newsletters or the local newspaper. Several websites specialize in supplying extensive lists of weeks for sale.

Many owners list their timeshares on Craigslist. However, since Craigslist is geographically organized, you may need to search across the entire site. Enter "timeshare site:Craigslist.org" as the Google search terms to look for timeshares across the regional sites.

Once you've found a seller, ask them for specific details about their week. Double check their facts, especially information they've provided in online ads that may contain old or incorrect information. Also, contact the resort to ask about upcoming special assessments and to verify the seller's claims.

Get all the facts in writing from the seller and ask questions if you don't understand some of their terminology. For example, know whether you're buying a deeded interest in the real estate or only a right to use membership. Discuss the terms you'll need for the purchase contract such as when the timeshare is available for first use and who's responsible for current maintenance fees. Remember, you're making a long term commitment. You're becoming an owner, so you need to understand what you are buying.

Research the seller so that you know who you're dealing with. If the seller is a company, check with the local Better Business Bureau and the NTOA. If it's an eBay seller, check the number of sales they've made and their reputation score. Use a Web search engine like Google to see if there are any online reports of issues with the seller. Unfortunately, some unscrupulous companies change names, making it difficult to track their reputation.

Table 6 provides a checklist of essential information to collect and understand before you purchase. You might want to photocopy the worksheet and fill it out for each week that you're considering. If possible, provide your questions to the seller in writing (such as in an e-mail) to help avoid miscommunication. Compare all provided answers to the terms in the purchase contract and the information in the estoppels letter (described later).

Determining the Value

As with any real estate, one of the toughest steps in buying a timeshare is finding a fair price that both the seller and the buyer **$** can agree upon. When you're buying a timeshare, a fair price is based on determining the value to you. However, your negotiating power will be influenced by supply and demand. Auctions provide a good value estimate because you know that there's currently at least one other person willing to pay almost as much as you are willing to pay (their next lower bid compared to your winning bid).

At some point, you'll probably want to sell or exchange your week. Therefore, it's important to consider how future potential buyers and exchange companies will value your week. Select a high quality property that will have high resale and exchange values. However, the exchange value should be secondary to your plans to use the timeshare.

Before purchasing a low-end week, consider that it will likely be difficult, if not impossible, to sell. Timeshares sell everyday on eBay for $1 because the owners want out and their weeks are not in high demand. Preferred lock-off units at high-end resorts with access to holiday weeks are more prized and their desirability makes them easier to sell.

The best weeks are often difficult to find for sale while low end weeks may literally be a dime a dozen. At the high end, some timeshare developers

Table 6. Purchase Worksheet

Ownership Type	Are you buying deeded ownership?	
	Are you buying points?	
	Is the resort part of a vacation club?	
Access / Using	Are you buying the right to use?	
	Is it a fixed week or floating time?	
	If you're buying floating time, when can you use your time (i.e., which seasons/weeks)?	
	How often can you access the resort (every year or every other year)?	
	When can you first use the week?	
	What's the reservation process?	
Exchanging	Which exchange company is the resort affiliated with (e.g., II, RCI)?	
	Does the resort offer internal exchanges?	
	Will you be receiving any bonus exchange weeks from the seller?	
Costs	What is the total purchase price?	
	Are there any additional incentives for buying from a developer?	
	What are the closing costs?	
	What are the maintenance fees?	
	Have the current year's maintenance fees and taxes already been paid?	
	How much are the taxes?	
	How much did maintenance fees increase this year?	
	Have any upcoming special assessments been announced?	
Process	What type of deed is being offered?	
	Who will be performing the closing process?	
	Will the agreement be documented in a contract?	
	How will money change hands?	

may ask over $100,000 for large units during peak weeks at new premier properties in places like Las Vegas, New York City, and Hawaii. At the low end, some owners are willing to literally give their units away to escape their commitment. You're more likely to find a motivated seller of a low value week, but you may not be happy with what you buy. If you're patient, you can find high end resale weeks available for reasonable prices.

Valuation Factors

Several factors affect the price and exchange value of a timeshare week. Many of the same factors that influence your purchase decision also affect the perceived value to others, and the price sellers ask. The primary factors impacting price are related to supply and demand: location, unit size/type, amenities, season, and effective age.

As with all real estate, location is critical. Location includes where the resort is located as well as where particular units are positioned within the resort's property. Subtle location factors make a significant difference in value. For example, a beach resort may have some units that are oceanfront while others are merely ocean view.

Most timeshare units have two bedrooms and many newer units are arranged as two bedroom lock-offs. One and three bedroom units are not unusual. Size is important not only for occupancy limits, but also to help compensate for noisy neighbors. Some flag shaped oceanfront units may be deeded as a double balcony versus a single balcony. Large units with a great deal of square feet are highly valued by those of us who enjoy a lot of space.

Amenities that significantly impact a resort's value include private golf courses and beach or ski-lift access. A lazy river feature in the pool area is a recent popular amenity. The relative value of amenities will depend on your personal interests.

The week's season, especially for fixed weeks, has a dramatic effect on desirability. The peak season at a ski resort may be allocated to fixed weeks. Hurricane season is much less popular in the southeast U.S. coast, Caribbean, and Cancun areas.

The effective age of the resort is a perceived value, which may be younger than the actual age because of improvements and renovations. Effective age is an important factor because some properties undergo major renovations that effectively reset or at least disguise the true age. Newer properties and renovated properties often have better finishes to appeal to buyers with higher expectations such as granite countertops and HDTVs.

Finding Comparables

Unlike year-round residential real estate, it's very difficult to find sales data on similar timeshare weeks to compare to asking prices. However, when you do find comparables, they're usually much closer than most traditional real estate property comparisons.

One source of sales data is the completed listings information on eBay that can be accessed using the advanced search option. Past sales on eBay are a good indicator but that information isn't available for very long after the auction. Some people track winning bids on eBay for months to understand what weeks are selling for at a resort they're considering. Make sure you're looking at completed listings that resulted in a sale and not the asking prices. Timeshares tend to sell more cheaply on eBay than from other sources and usually aren't high end resorts or prime weeks. However, you may find it a beneficial site for gaining insight into timeshare market comparables.

Resist the temptation to use developer asking prices and advertised prices as a basis for determining value. Remember, developer prices cover high overhead costs, including compensating the sales staff and funding marketing efforts. Unfortunately, many owners have no idea that their week cannot be sold for what they paid a developer. Sellers often have unrealistic expectations of their week's value, but that should not bias your own perception of a week's value.

You may be able to figure out what buyers have been paying for deeded timeshares by looking at public records online, especially when they have associated loans that are recorded in public records. This usually occurs when charter owners purchase from developers.

Maintenance Fees as a Basis for Valuation

Compare a timeshare's rental cost to its maintenance fees as one indicator of its value. Look at the resort's website to determine what the unit costs to rent during your preferred season. Also, check owners' rental ads and auctions. If the rent is less than the maintenance fees, there's currently no advantage in buying. In that situation, consider merely renting instead of purchasing. By renting, you don't have to lock yourself into a commitment to enjoy the ongoing use of the accommodations. If rents rise or rentals aren't readily available in the future, it may become more advantageous to buy a week. Also, you may be assigned a better unit as an owner.

Other Purchase Costs

When you're considering price, don't forget that there are typically additional costs associated with buying a timeshare. The seller normally pays any broker fees. However, the buyer usually pays expenses including closing costs (including recording fees and transfer fees), maintenance fees, and finance costs. However, desperate sellers sometimes offer to pay some or all of the closing costs and offer other incentives to encourage a sale.

The primary driver of closing costs is whether a closing agency is used. You can choose to perform the closing process yourself, but it's usually best to have the professionals transfer the funds and record the deed. Closing companies usually charge a few hundred dollars (usually $300-$600).

The closing company may offer you title insurance. Although some people choose to purchase title insurance it's rarely necessary for timeshare purchases. Since the value of the underlying asset is relatively small and the deeds are fairly simple, you probably won't need title insurance the way you would with a house.

As real estate, deeded timeshare transactions are recorded in local government public records. Recording fees vary depending on the resort's location. Take the time to educate yourself on the local jurisdiction's processes and fees. For example, because of some of the unique laws in Hawaii extra costs are sometimes incurred. Also, count on transfer fees, an administrative cost paid to the resort to change their records. These fees typically cost around $100.

Depending on the timing of your timeshare purchase and your agreement with the seller, there may be maintenance fees or special assessments that are due for the unit, which the resort will expect to be paid when the ownership is transferred. Typically, the buyer only pays to reimburse the seller for a maintenance fees already paid for a week that is still available for use in the coming year.

Some people finance the purchase of their timeshare, especially when they're buying from a developer. The interest rates for these loans are often very high. One of the advantages of buying resale is that the price is low enough that you should be able to pay cash for a low price instead of borrowing money to purchase an expensive week from a developer.

Negotiating and Documenting the Price and Terms

Once you've valued the week, try to stay below your figure when negotiating with the seller or placing a bid in an auction. Unlike other types of real estate, it's highly probable that a very similar timeshare week will become available.

The method you use for negotiating the price and making an offer depends on the way the current owner is selling the week. The seller may signal their motivation level by using an auction for a fast sale or patiently listing it with a broker. If possible, base your offer price on a reference point, such as a recent eBay completed auction.

Think about the total cost of ownership before you make an offer. Consider the purchase price, closing costs, ongoing and escalating maintenance fees, and possible special assessments. Maintenance fees will likely increase – probably around the rate of inflation each year. Additionally, expect special assessments to come up every few years, especially with older and beachfront properties.

Make sure you understand what you're buying and perform your due diligence. You're making a long term commitment and it might not be easy to escape that obligation. For the foreseeable future, it's a buyer's market, so don't rush into any decisions. Once you've negotiated the price and terms, document them in a written contract.

Negotiating with a Developer

If you're buying from a developer, you're likely dealing with a well-trained sales team that is motivated to complete a transaction quickly. A professional sales person will patiently explain how their system works. Even if you repeatedly say "no", you're likely to be passed off to a series of other salespeople who will try to convince you to buy that day. You may find that the price drops with each sales person you talk to as they hand you off to others and magically discover suddenly available discounts and cheaper inventory. Don't allow them to pressure you or rush your decision. Stay alert and refrain from consuming alcohol before or during the sales presentation.

Responding to an Owner's Advertisement

Responding to an owner's advertisement is the first step in negotiating an offer on a resale timeshare. Don't appear too interested. Try to get a sense of how anxious the seller is to dispose of their week. If there's a large supply and desperate sellers, one strategy is to offer an extremely low price. You run the risk of insulting the seller, but it may help you obtain a lower price. Most sellers will counter your offer with another price if they're unwilling to accept your first offer. Another strategy is to carefully time your offer. Consider making your offer in the late Fall when sellers face maintenance fee bills and your competitors are distracted by the holidays.

Base your offer on something tangible such as recent sales on eBay. Disclose to the sellers the basis for your offer. Don't let the seller use asking prices on websites as the foundation of your negotiations. Those prices are often posted by advertising companies for uninformed sellers and they represent unsold weeks. Your offer may serve as a reality check to an owner, in terms of the going rate for their week, especially if they paid a retail price to a developer. It may take them some time to realize that your price is fair. As long as you trust the seller, there's no reason not to buy from the owner offering the lowest price.

Bidding in an Auction

Timeshares sometimes show up at charity auctions. However, on line sites like eBay are more typical auction forums. Beware of error-filled auction listings for timeshares on these sites. For example, you may discover an old maintenance fee amount listed instead of the current amount. Ask the seller clarifying questions and don't bid on the item unless you receive acceptable answers and plan to consummate the transaction. Decide ahead of time what you're willing to pay and bid as late in the process as possible with your maximum bid. Some bidders wait until the very end of an auction to place their bid so that others won't have time to decide whether to raise their bid. This strategy is called sniping. Sniping software is available that will help you place extremely last minute bids.

Documenting the Agreement in a Contract

Use a written contract to document your agreement on the price and terms of the transaction. The contract should specifically identify the type of timeshare, when you'll first have access to it, what payments must be made, and when. If you're the one creating the contract, obtain a sample online or from the NTOA.

Timeshare sales contracts in the United States are regulated by state law. For example, in Florida, specific wording must appear in the contracts. An improper contract may invalidate the purchase. Whether buying from a developer or resale, get the details of your agreement in writing and make copies of the contract. Take note of the contract date for rescission purposes.

Completing the Purchase

Once you've successfully negotiated a fair price with the seller, you must legally take ownership of the timeshare. For deeded timeshares, this means transferring title. It may take weeks or months to go through the process for resale weeks. However, developer purchases are usually completed more quickly. The process may be supported by a closing company or handled by the buyer and seller. The purchase of a deeded timeshare is a real estate transaction that should conform to a process that includes a written contract, estoppels letter, deed, and transfer (for resale). Since the closing process may be lengthy, take the schedule into account when planning to use or trade the week. The process for closing the purchase depends on the type of timeshare (deeded or RTU) and the laws where the timeshare is located.

Closing Deeded Timeshares

The deeded timeshare closing process involves recording the deed with the local government, paying recording fees, and transferring ownership with the resort. A deed transfers title from the previous owner to you. Insist on using a closing agent if you're buying a resale timeshare and you're not totally convinced that the seller is capable of performing the process correctly. Brokers typically arrange for a closing company to support the closing process. If you need help finding a closing company, organizations such as the NTOA can provide referrals.

Since timeshare purchases are so much smaller than single family home transactions, their deeds often receive less attention. As a result, timeshares sometimes have title problems. The risk of title issues may also be higher with timeshares since they may be resold many times.

If you buy title insurance, the closing company performs a title search as part of issuing the title insurance policy. Title insurance protects the buyer from title defects, liens, and unpaid maintenance fees, up to the amount of the purchase price. However, it probably doesn't make sense to buy title insurance for a timeshare unless you're buying a high priced unit and the insurance would provide you needed peace of mind. Since the insurance only protects up to the purchase price, which is likely small if you're buying resale, consider forgoing the title insurance.

The closing company prepares documents pertaining to the transfer, including the deed. They also provide escrow services by holding the buyer's funds and then dispersing them to the seller upon completion of the transaction. This helps mitigate financial transaction risks. Professional sellers on eBay usually use a closing company that they identify along with estimating closing costs in the auction listing. Figure 9 shows how the relationship between the involved entities may occur.

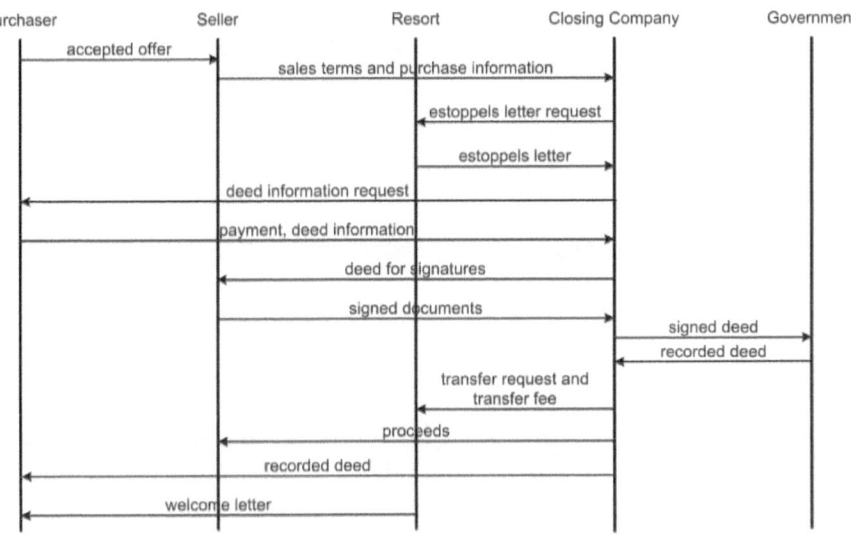

**Figure 9. Deeded Timeshare Closing Handled
by a Closing Company**

You don't have to employ a closing company to process the paperwork. If you're buying from someone you know and you're confident that they can perform the process correctly, you might want to save money by completing the process together instead of employing a closing company. Deeded timeshare closings include recording the deed with the local government. If you're recording the deed yourself, find out the process from the county where the resort is located. They'll likely require a completed form, original deed with notarized signatures, and a recording fee. Some people obtain a copy of the current deed from the seller and use it to create a new document, replacing the old names with the new names.

They'll add their tracking numbers, scan the deed, and return the recorded document to you when they are finished. Figure 10 shows how the process may occur between the involved entities when the buyer and seller perform the transfer without a closing company.

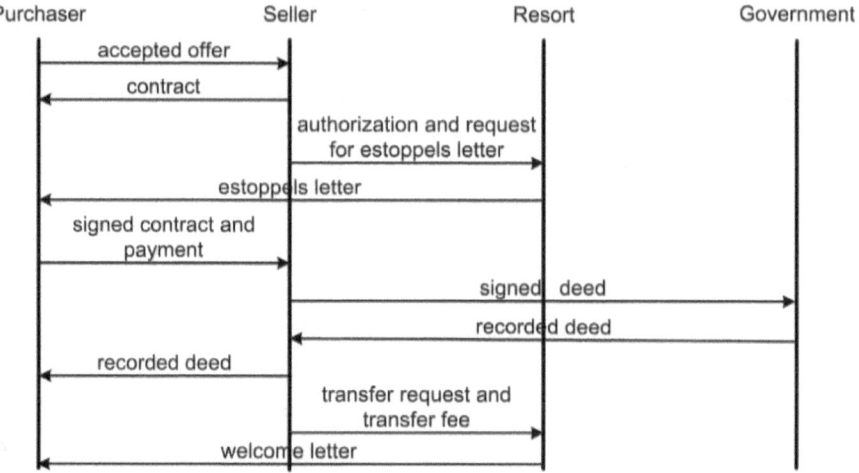

Figure 10. Deeded Timeshare Closing Handled by Involved Parties

The seller should mail or fax a letter to the resort informing them of the impending ownership change. The resort may have a form to be completed and use the information to assign the new owner a contract or membership number. They'll likely charge a small transfer fee (around $100) to update their records. There may be an additional charge for the buyer to obtain a copy of the legal documents that describe the timeshare plan and HOA.

Closing RTU Timeshares

If you buy a points membership or additional points in a system that you already participate in, you'll record the purchase with the company that operates the program. The seller's RTU contract should specify how to transfer their ownership to you as the new owner. Expect to complete some forms and to pay a transfer fee. You might also have to pay an additional fee if you're joining the points system for the first time with your RTU purchase. The closing costs for a points-based RTU timeshare purchase may depend on the number of points that you buy.

Right of First Refusal (ROFR) Option

Some timeshare developers retain a Right of First Refusal (ROFR) option that gives them the right to match the resale price that a seller may have negotiated with a buyer. ROFR rules must be specified in your contract or program documents. Developers sometimes exercise their option if the price is low enough and they want the week back to try and resell it at a higher price.

People debate the motivation for using the ROFR option. Some believe that developers use ROFR to try and maintain a minimum resale price which in turn helps them justify their high prices. Developers may also use their ROFR option to buy weeks at low prices to resell without having to compete in the open market. However, developers may be less interested in building up their inventory of weeks for sale than they are in maintaining the flow of maintenance fees from owned weeks.

An ROFR option affects the closing process. The resort must choose whether or not to exercise ROFR before the sale can be completed. Therefore, an ROFR clause can complicate, delay, or disrupt the sale, especially if the option owner takes too long to exercise or decline their right. Find out if the week that you want to buy is subject to an ROFR clause. If it is, the seller must communicate with the developer and obtain a sales contract with them or a Letter of Declination that documents the option owner's decision to waive their right of first refusal. The Letter of Declination may be required for properly closing the transaction.

The impact of the ROFR clause is debatable. ROFR primarily benefits the developer by providing them access to units to resell for less than it costs to build them. Although some people view ROFR as a helpful tool to keep resale prices stable, there is no guarantee that the developer will exercise their option to purchase the week at a low resale price. A ROFR option can result in artificially higher prices for resale buyers and doesn't help sellers at all as frustrated buyers who have to jump through this extra hoop may be inclined to purchase elsewhere.

Estoppels Letter

Before you buy a timeshare, make sure that the owners own what they think they do and that they're current on their maintenance fees and special assessments. A document called an estoppels letter communicates the resort's understanding of the seller's status based on their records.

An estoppels letter reassures the buyer regarding facts associated with a week being purchased. It describes ownership and provides the current status of maintenance fee and special assessment payments.

Only an owner or their closing company can authorize the resort to provide an estoppels letter to the buyer. The resort might not provide an estoppels letter without permission from the seller to release the information. If you're helping perform the closing yourself, you may want to prepare a permission letter for the seller to sign and send to the resort. The estoppels letter will be sent to the requester. If you're using a closing company, ask them for a copy of the letter.

The fairly simple letter identifies the unit and week owned. It should also indicate the next time the unit can be used (sometimes called the use year). All the information in the estoppels letter should match the purchase contract terms. Also, be sure to check the name and address of the resort. Many properties have very similar names and resellers can get them confused, so double check the resort name and address that they provide in the estoppels letter. The estoppels letter varies by resort but should be dated and identify the items shown in Table 7.

Table 7. Estoppels Letter Contents

Information	Example Values
Owner's name in records (may differ from deed)	John Q. Owner
Maintenance fees associated with ownership	$700/year
Unpaid maintenance fees and special assessments	$0
Outstanding loan balance	$0
Next maintenance fee due date	12/1/2012
Deeded unit/week or number of points	710 / Week 52
Floating information (e.g., unit type, restrictions)	light red float
Next available use	1/1/2013
Whether week is subject to Right of First Refusal	no

Program Documents

If you want to be very thorough, obtain a copy of the official program documents from the seller or the resort in order to gather more details. The resort may charge for copies and might only release the documents to existing owners, so you may have to request them from the seller if you're buying a resale week. By reviewing the documents, you can compare them to what was represented in the advertisement or sales presentation.

Payment

If you use a closing company, they escrow the funds. However, paying a closing company may not be worth mitigating the risk of a small transaction not being properly completed. For example, if you buy a $250 timeshare, you may want to take your chances and send a check directly to the seller. Consider sending a cashier's check or a money order so that the seller doesn't have to wait for your check to clear before they continue with the transfer process.

Deed Preparation

Traditional timeshares are often deeded to their owners like a home is deeded to its owners. Point-based timeshare purchases are essentially long term leases. Warranty deeds and quitclaim deeds are the two most common types of deeds used for timeshares. A warranty deed warrants that the owner has the legal rights to the title. A quitclaim deed states that the owner is no longer making any claims to the property. Deeds typically require notarized signatures from the sellers.

The timeshare deed lists the names of its new owners. Carefully consider which names you want to place on the deed because the names on a timeshare deed may affect privileges for exchanging and day use. You might want to use the name of a trust or the trustees of your trust on the deed. If you already own timeshares identified within an exchange company account, you may need to be consistent with the names you already use to exchange multiple weeks without paying for another exchange company account. Using multiple names on a deed, such as the names of your children or siblings, may provide access to the named individuals without paying guest fees when you're not with them. Also consider whether to specify joint ownership with rights of survivorship.

Recording the Deed

Deed recording processes vary with local laws. Check with the government office where the resort is located. They may have a website with recording instructions and an explanation of costs and acceptable forms of payment. Make copies of the deed before you mail it to the recording office. Send the original (not a copy) with notarized signatures. Include payment for the recording fees. Include a cover letter that indicates the address where the recorded deed should be sent. Once you receive the recorded deed, check online to ensure that the deed was recorded correctly in the public records database.

Resort Transfer

The week's owners' names and contact information must be changed in the management company's and the HOA's records. You may need to submit a form and provide a copy of the recorded deed to the resort. Most resorts require a transfer fee to process the change. The resort may send a welcome kit to new owners, or provide a password to access the owners-only portion of their website.

Obtain a copy of the program documents from the seller or the resort. Read and understand these documents that describe how your timeshare operates. The rules of the timeshare may be documented in by-laws, covenants, declarations, and rule books that describe upgrade policies, calendars, day use privileges, reservation policies, and internal exchange options.

The resort transfer process must be completed before you can reserve and use your week. If the closing company was supposed to pay maintenance fees, contact the resort to make sure they've been paid.

Rescinding - The Cure for Buyer's Remorse

Remorse following the transaction. As with any major purchasing decision, buyers often experience remorse. Most states have laws that grant timeshare purchasers the option for backing out called rescinding. This legal right provides a cooling-off period. You can rescind for any reason immediately after the purchase. Sometimes a buyer rescinds after they've had time to reconsider the purchase and determines that the purchase was unwise in terms of price paid, whether they can afford it, and whether it makes sense for them. Hopefully, this thought process occurs outside of the emotion of the sales presentation or the excitement of an auction.

Some purchasers realize they've overpaid a developer and that they can buy the same timeshare on the resale market at a substantially discounted price. Others recognize that they made a spontaneous emotional decision. Some buyers become defensive about their purchase because they don't want to be embarrassed about their decision.

Buyers have a limited number of days to cancel their contract. Depending on your state, the law may apply to resale timeshares as well as timeshares sold by developers. You should be able to rescind even if you promised the salesperson you wouldn't (or as has happened in Mexico – you sign something waiving your right to rescind).

The contracts documents should include instructions for the rescission process. Follow these instructions to the letter. Keep copies of everything and obtain proof of delivery such as confirmation pages for faxes and return receipts for certified letters.

The seller may ask you to return or pay for your copies of program documents that you received when you purchased. When the rescission process is completed, the seller should return any monies you already paid.

Alternatives to Buying

Take your time to educate yourself, perform research, and think about making the decision to buy a timeshare, especially from a developer. There are other ways to enjoy high quality resort accommodations with less cost and commitment. Many options exist with timeshares including access approaches and ownership models. However, you probably won't receive information on all your options from sales presentations targeted for a particular resort or system.

Before you get caught up in the excitement of buying a timeshare, consider alternative approaches for securing resort accommodations. For example, you can rent timeshare units or stay at hotels that provide suites with kitchen facilities.

Renting a timeshare unit is a great commitment-free option. If you're renting directly from an owner, make sure that they have the right to rent out the unit. For example, they should not rent you a week they received from an exchange company. Try to verify their right to rent with the resort. Document your agreement in a lease or simple contract that specifies the terms and conditions – especially payment and cancellation options. Ask for a reservation confirmation letter from the resort with your name on it. You can also rent directly from the resort, or possibly from an exchange company.

Many hotel companies now offer suites. Some suites may include kitchens with appliances you would expect to find at a timeshare. These hotels usually provide typical hotel-like services, but cater to guests that have extended stays compared to typical short stay hotels. You have much more flexibility in your travel arrangements because you don't have to stay for seven days and you don't have to arrive and depart on a particular day of the week.

Timeshare Purchase Summary

Remember that when you're buying a timeshare, you're making a long term commitment. Decide what's important to you, and then find a timeshare resort that meets your criteria. Consider buying resale instead of buying directly from the developer to save money. Decide what the timeshare is worth and make an offer. One reason that buying resale is so much less expensive is that there are many owners anxious to terminate their commitment and get out of their timeshare. This gives you incredible negotiating power. Document your agreement to buy the timeshare with a contract. Make sure you want to buy the timeshare before the rescission period ends. Don't rush into purchasing a timeshare. Educate yourself prior to making the long term commitment.

The best part about owning a timeshare is using it with your friends and family. You have a week to relax, have fun, and make memories. You then have a year to look forward to your next getaway. If you've bought or inherited a timeshare, get as much value as you can out of your ownership. Maximize your timeshare use by  carefully planning, reserving your week (if you don't have a fixed week), enjoying your time at the resort, and staying involved. Owning a week may involve other activities throughout the year, including participation in the HOA and enjoying day use privileges. You might also enjoy a week you obtain from an exchange company through a trade or by renting. The primary reason for owning a timeshare should be to regularly enjoy using a unit at either your home resort or another desirable location.

Maximizing Your Enjoyment

Amazingly, some people buy a timeshare and hardly ever use their week. When you own a timeshare, get the most out of your ownership. After all, enjoying your timeshare is the reason you bought it. You want to experience all the features that influenced your purchase decision. With careful planning, you'll feel like you obtain value as you create memories for a lifetime.

Use Options

As with any type of vacationing or traveling, timeshare use requires careful planning. It pays to plan ahead. The earlier out you make your plans, the more options will be available. The annual nature of timesharing may force you to plan and take a vacation. Each year, you'll make decisions on what to do with your week. Options include using it for a whole week getaway, working at least part time from the timeshare (including telecommuting), participating in a co-located event, splitting the week, or even, depending on how many units you own, moving from one timeshare to the next.

Traditionally, people stayed at timeshare resorts for an entire week. However, many owners use only a portion of their week. Depending on your check-in day and the resort's distance from your home, you may wind up arriving after the check-in time or leaving before the required check-out deadline.

Many timeshares provide Internet access that can be used for entertainment or work. Some of us now have jobs that provide the opportunity to work remotely. Combining tele-commuting with flexible work schedules may provide you the opportunity to work from your timeshare at least part of the week. Although you don't get to enjoy the resort the whole time, at least you're getting paid to work at a great location, which helps with the costs of the vacation.

Timeshares can provide convenient lodging for special events such as weddings, family reunions, or business conferences. Once you know that you need to be at a particular location on a certain date, you can try and find a unit to rent or exchange into.

Some deeded resorts allow you to split your week into a four day period and a three day period for a small charge. If you're not too far away from the resort, this may provide you with two mini-vacations. Most points systems already have this type of flexibility built in.

There are even people who buy several timeshares and use, rent, and exchange in order to spend most of the year at resorts! You may not be prepared to spend that much time away, but it is possible if you rent or buy additional weeks.

Usage Process

Using your timeshare involves more than merely showing up once a year at the resort. You've made an on-going financial commitment that must be fulfilled. Unless you're a fixed week owner, you'll need to make reservations. You can improve your experience through careful planning. Once you've arrived and settled in, you can enjoy the unit, the resort, and the local area until your use time ends and you depart. You can then stay connected with the resort throughout the year. Figure 11 summarizes this process for using your timeshare.

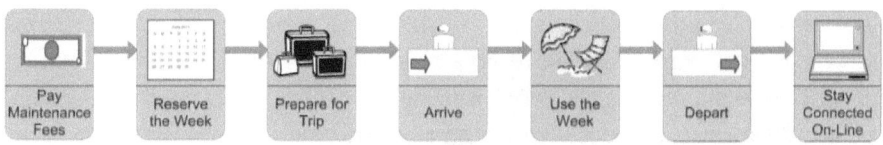

Figure 11. Use Process

Fulfilling Your On-Going Financial Responsibilities

Even if you don't use your week, you must still pay your share of the costs of operating and maintaining the resort. A great advantage of timesharing over sole ownership is that someone else handles the maintenance issues to keep the property operating and periodically makes repairs and improvements. The resort collects annual maintenance fees and occasional special assessments from the owners to fund these efforts. Both maintenance fees and special assessments must be up to date before you use your week or deposit it for exchange.

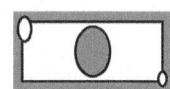

Operation and Maintenance Expenses

As with any real estate, there are costs associated with operating and maintaining a resort. The property requires periodic repair and replacement of items that break or wear out. The resort must also save up for large anticipated expenses such as reroofing by establishing reserve funds. Property taxes for the resort must also be shared by the owners. The owners share the responsibility of paying the resort's annual expenses including operating costs, reserves, and property taxes.

Operating expenses pay for the daily operation of the resort including management, maintenance, housekeeping, utilities, and insurance. Expenses for timeshares vary greatly depending on how the resort is managed. Some resorts pay a management fee to a company that pays many of the staffing expenses, while other resorts hire their staff directly. Labor costs, including salaries, payroll taxes, and benefits for the front desk, back office, maintenance, and housekeeping staffs often represent the largest operating expense.

Reserve funds are like savings accounts funded by annual contributions to satisfy state mandated requirements for covering large expenses and capital costs that only occur every few years. Resorts save money in separate reserve accounts to prepare for these major anticipated expenses.

The resort should share the status of these accounts with the owners in a reserve schedule report. The reserve schedule lists the major long lasting expensive items such as the roof, parking lot paving, equipment, painting, air conditioning, and the swimming pool that will eventually need to be replaced.

Reserves are also used for periodic furnishing refreshment like new furniture and appliances. The reserve schedule also shows the estimated number of years remaining before the replacement or repair is necessary. The anticipated lifetime should be determined by an engineering study.

Budgets

Each year, resorts plan for all the anticipated expenses for the upcoming year. The spending plans serve as the basis for determining required maintenance fees. The HOA approves budgets with expense sections related to planned expenditures and revenue sections that identify the source of funds to pay those expenses. The annual budget is normally mailed out to all owners.

The annual budget, which includes ongoing costs, reserve calculations, and taxes, dictates the maintenance fee and property tax assessments that owners must pay. Initially set by the developer, the HOA BoD eventually retains control over determining maintenance fees. After the HOA prepares a budget and estimates reserve requirements and property tax amounts, they set the fees while simultaneously balancing cost containment for owners and maintaining the owners' resort.

Some states regulate timeshare financial reporting. For example, in Florida, the state with the most timeshares, the law requires timeshares to file copies of their budgets with the state within a month of approval by the HOA BoD. State laws may also require that reserve funds and normal operating funds be maintained in separate accounts. Reserves should not be transferred into the normal operating fund account without approval by the owners.

Revenues

Resorts collect revenues to pay all of the identified expenses, fund the reserves, and pay the property taxes. Most of a timeshare's revenues come from maintenance fee assessments and special assessments. However, a resort might receive other miscellaneous income such as late fees.

Maintenance Fees

Maintenance fees provide the largest source of income for the HOA managing the resort. The HOA typically assesses owners annually for their share of operating expenses, reserves for major expenses, and property taxes. Some people think of maintenance fees as annual dues. Maintenance fees are the largest on-going cost of owning and using your week, with the possible exception of airfare for large groups traveling to distant resorts. Maintenance fees typically range from $600-$1200 per year.

Maintenance fees are not locked in at a particular amount. Instead, they typically increase annually. The maintenance fees may go up every year in order to cover depreciation and inflation. However, at some point, the maintenance fees may exceed the rental cost for accessing a unit at the resort, eliminating a key financial benefit of ownership.

Rising maintenance fees are one of the biggest causes of dissatisfaction among owners. Although maintenance fees might seem undesirable, someone needs to pay to keep the resort maintained and operating. It's to your advantage for the resort to be professionally maintained and staffed. Consistently maintaining the resort's quality and services will help you to use or sell the timeshare in a similar condition to when you bought your week. These fees would be more expensive if resorts provided hotel-level amenities including daily housekeeping and room service.

Each owner's share of the maintenance fees are allocated based on their ownership percentage, their unit's square footage, or the size of the unit. For example, one bedroom unit owners may pay less than three bedroom unit owners. With points systems, the owning entity may calculate your maintenance fees on a per-point basis that is tied to your home resort. Although sales ads normally disclose maintenance fees, make sure the listed amount in the advertisement reflects the current annual assessment.

Developers sometimes keep maintenance fees artificially low while they're actively selling weeks. If the developer subsidized your maintenance fees when you purchased your week, count on those fees increasing dramatically once the HOA takes control of the resort.

Most resorts inform owners of upcoming maintenance fees by sending a copy of the approved budget showing how the maintenance fees will be spent and how they were calculated. The fees may be billed monthly or annually. Because biennial owners only access their units half as often as yearly owners do, they usually receive prorated maintenance fees equaling half the monthly or annual amount.

Maintenance fee bills may include property taxes or they may be billed separately. Pay your maintenance fees on time to avoid late fees and interest or from being prevented from using your week. Paying on time helps the resort's cash flow situation and helps minimize borrowing expenses that get passed along to owners. Use a credit card if possible to gain perks (as long as you don't carry a balance that causes interest charges). Some companies allow you to spread annually billed maintenance fees over multiple payments.

Special Assessments

In addition to ongoing expenses, the controlling entity or HOA BoD may impose special assessments to cover unplanned costs. This occurs under unique situations such as unforeseen repairs or natural disasters that result in expenses that cannot be covered under the normal maintenance fees, funded reserves, or insurance. The odds of this happening may be higher with coastal properties affected by hurricanes and older properties requiring major repairs.

Tax Consequences

The portion of your maintenance fees that cover your share of expenses and reserves are not deductible on your taxes. If you own a business, you cannot deduct timeshare-related costs because a timeshare is considered an entertainment facility which doesn't qualify as a business deduction. However, your share of the property taxes and any mortgage interest you pay might be deductible. Check with your tax professional if you're unsure.

If you itemize your taxes, check to see if you qualify for deducting your portion of the property taxes. In order to deduct the property taxes, they must be invoiced on a separate bill or identified separately from operating costs and reserves on the maintenance fee bill. The timeshare budget documents alone might not be considered an auditable source of the amount used for tax filing purposes.

Most timeshare loans are structured as personal loans, not mortgages secured by the timeshare as collateral. However, if you do pay timeshare mortgage loan interest, it might be deductible under certain circumstances.

Reserving Use Time

If you don't own a fixed week, you need to reserve your time at the resort each year. Weekly timeshare use is tied to weeks of the year beginning on a particular day of the week called the check-in day. For example, some timeshare ownerships have a Saturday check-in and some have a Sunday check-in every year. Timeshare calendars that identify the check-in date for a particular week number each year are readily available online and in exchange company literature. The calendar dates depend on the week, year, check-in day of the week, and the resort.

One popular set of calendar dates is provided in Appendix B. However, confirm your dates with your resort or exchange company because their calendars may be different. Because of leap year, there is an extra week on the timeshare calendar every four years. Reservations are usually only needed for floating weeks and point-based systems, not fixed weeks. However, the resort may ask how you plan on using your fixed week.

Floating Week Reservations

Floating week owners aren't restricted to a particular (fixed) week and must reserve their usage, usually within a restricted subset of weeks. Resorts use different floating time approaches. For example, a ski resort might have one group of ski weeks and a Florida beach property might have another set of floating weeks associated with school holidays. The most prized floating weeks are those that are unrestricted and can be used any time of the year (weeks 1-52).

Reserving a floating week is similar to booking a hotel room online or over the phone. Resorts allow owners to begin making reservations at some point prior (often 12 months earlier) to the desired check-in day. The earlier you make your reservation, the better the odds that your first choice will still be available. Some resorts use a lottery-type system to handle competing requests for high demand weeks.

Floating Week Reservation Process

Make sure you understand the reservation rules to increase the likelihood of getting your desired week. Some resorts waive certain reservation restrictions such as use week restrictions, unit size, and unit view if you pay an upgrade fee. Other properties allow you to split your seven days into a four day and a three day period for a small fee.

First, decide on your date preferences and backup dates. Think about which week you'll want well in advance. Perhaps you want your stay to coincide with the school calendar, work holidays, or an event you'll be attending such as a family reunion or conference. You might want to reserve a week during a high demand period for your resort if you plan on renting out or exchanging your week. Submit your reservation as early as possible. Depending on the resort, you may be able to request a particular view, unit, or floor when you make the reservation. Even if the resort can't guarantee your request, they may record your desires in the computer and consider them when they're assigning units. Request a written confirmation of your reservation.

Inform the resort of your anticipated arrival date and time. At some resorts, late check-ins can result in forfeiture of your right to use your week. If you allow a friend or relative to use your week for free or rent out your week, inform the resort that someone else is using your unit and provide their contact information.

Points Reservations

Points owners reserve the resort and time they want to use. The reservation timeframe window may open earlier for staying at their home resort than alternative locations. The number of points needed to make a reservation depends on the resort, dates (season), check-in day of the week, length of stay, and unit size. Points systems provide members with directories and charts that indicate how many points are needed for each type of reservation.

Preparing to Use Your Week.

As you plan to use your week, carefully consider all aspects of your travel arrangements. As with any vacation, the anticipation of using your timeshare and planning for your time away represents half the fun.

Fixed Weeks Use Intentions

Fixed week owners already know when they're week is available. Some people enjoy the comfort, consistency, and knowledge that they'll have the same week each year. Some owners like to know that they're guaranteed especially high demand weeks such as Christmas and New Year's weeks most years. Even if you own a fixed week, let the resort know whether you plan to use, share, exchange, or rent out your week.

Planning

If you're flying to your resort, check with the resort for transportation options to see if you'll need to rent a car, or if you can use shuttles or public transportation to get to and from the airport and around the local area.

Call or e-mail the resort to confirm your reservation before you leave home to avoid surprises at check-in. Contact the resort at least a week prior to your arrival date with your confirmation number (if you have one). Use the confirmation contact as an opportunity to request a particular unit type, location, or view within the resort. Also, provide the resort with any special requests such as renting a playpen. Some resorts assign guests to units at the time of the reservation while others wait until closer to arrival time. The resort may select a particular unit for you based on whether you're an owner, renter, or exchanger.

Packing

Check the weather so you'll know what activities you'll likely participate in and what types of clothing to pack. Some people treat the trip like a hotel vacation – taking only their clothes and toiletries, while others treat timesharing more like camping and bring everything but the kitchen sink.

Timeshare vacations require a different approach to packing than hotel stays. Unlike hotels, many timeshares do not provide soap and shampoo, so bring your own or put them on your shopping list. Many timeshares provide a starter kit with basics. However, it's always a good idea to bring anything that you think you might need that might not be readily available at or near the resort. If you're driving, it's easy to bring many items. However, if you're flying, keep in mind the airline's baggage weight limits and fees as well as carry-on restrictions.

Many timeshare owners enjoy having a fully equipped kitchen for cooking. If you plan on using the unit's kitchen, consider packing your favorite cooking-related items. Bring along things that don't make sense to buy for a week's use such as an ice cream scoop or spices for recipes. Pack a shopping list and recipes so that you'll be prepared for your visit to the grocery store. A few resorts allow you to preorder groceries from their on-site store and deliver them to your unit before you arrive. If you don't like washing dishes while on vacation, buy disposable dishes and utensils. A Sharpie marker is handy for writing names on disposable cups in order to reuse them. Individual packets of condiments also come in handy. If you live close to the resort, you may want to take a cooler for bringing home leftover food at the end of the week.

Don't forget to pack for entertainment activities. Bring your sports equipment such as tennis rackets and golf clubs, especially if your resort does not lend or rent these items. Some resorts rent DVDs and lend puzzles and books but take your own for a rainy day if you prefer. Check with your cell phone company regarding extra roaming fees or if you need to activate additional features for international travel. Bring a highlighter to mark the activities schedule and Post-it notes to flag restaurant ads in local travel guides. As with any vacation, make preparations before you leave home. Stop the paper and the mail so that it looks like you're home. Most timeshares don't allow pets, so make arrangements for their care. The resort may fine you if you bring a pet into your unit.

Arriving

Make sure you know when and where to check in when you arrive at the resort as the front desk may be located in a different location or in a separate building from the one housing your unit. If you're going to arrive late at a resort without a 24 hour front desk, make arrangements for access to your unit. Some resorts use lock boxes to leave you the keys. They may provide you a combination code to access the lock box. Ultimately, owning a timeshare leads to you and your friends and family enjoying the use of your week. Spending a week at a timeshare can become a comfortable routine that starts with checking in, moving in, settling in, and getting oriented.

Checking In

Many resorts maintain a single check-in and check-out day. Therefore, the resort's housekeeping staff may have only a few hours to clean units vacated earlier on the day you arrive. Respect the front desk staff and recognize how busy that day is for their resort. Some resorts will pre-register you early in the day and then call you when your unit's been cleaned and is ready for your use.

Understand all the rules and procedures of the property. Rules can affect everything including towel exchange, trash removal, maintenance requests, cleanings, minimum age to check-in, and maximum number of occupants. Expect fines if you exceed the maximum number of occupants. Not only do extra guests add to the wear and tear of the unit, but they may violate the fire codes. If you're checking in as an exchanger or renter, be prepared to provide a copy of your reservation confirmation and a credit card as a security deposit. Owners may also need a credit card to open a charge account for the resort's bar or restaurant.

Some resorts use key cards with magnetic stripes that provide access to the units and can also be used to charge items to the room. Keep those keys away from devices like cell phones that may accidentally demagnetize them. Additionally, you may receive keys that open a pool gate or access areas such as a laundry room or trash chute. You may be provided a limited number of bracelets that display your access rights to restricted areas such as the pool or beach. The number of bracelets you receive is determined by the number of occupants in your unit. You may need an access code for the parking garage or gates to the beach or pool. Distribute keys and access codes to the rest of your party and discuss who'll be responsible for incurred charges. Place shared keys in an agreed-upon location in the unit.

Moving In

When you are ready to bring your belongings into the unit, look for a luggage cart, recognizing that they may have been left on other floors. Be sure to return the carts you use to the check-in area when you're through unloading them.

Before you bring your luggage into the unit, consider taking pictures to use later for advertising your unit for rent or sale. It's better to take your photos before you clutter the unit with your belongings. The pictures may also help you remember the furniture layout so that you can return anything you move to its proper place before you leave.

Inspect the unit before you unpack. Make sure it's clean and does not have any obvious maintenance issues. If you don't like something about the unit, go back to the front desk immediately and ask for the problem to be remedied or for a different unit. Timeshare occupancy levels are typically much higher than at a hotel, so they may not have other units available. Furthermore, your unit type may be dictated based on what you bought or exchanged into. If the resort cannot move you, make sure they know that you expect them to quickly resolve the issue.

Setting Up

Many timeshares provide an inventory list of everything that should be in your unit. Take some time to inspect the rooms and complete the inventory. While it probably isn't necessary to count every fork in the kitchen cabinet drawers, look around for any obviously missing items and report them to the front desk.

Many two bedroom units have twin beds in the second bedroom. If you'd prefer a king bed configuration, you may be able to move the beds together and connect them with straps (sold online) and cover them with a king sheet. Some resorts provide the king sheets and combine the beds for you upon request, but at others you may need to bring an extra set of king size bed sheets with you.

Fill the ice trays or check to make sure that the ice maker is turned on. Some people like to run all the dishes and utensils through the dishwasher when they arrive to make sure that they're clean. Spray air freshener on the carpets and linens upon arrival if you want the unit to smell better.

Many people like to fully unpack into dressers and closets, especially for a week-long stay. If you brought a computer or mobile device and the resort offers an Internet connection, connect and make sure everything's working properly. Certain areas of the resort or your unit may have better Wi-Fi and cell phone coverage than others.

Orienting Yourself

Look around the unit for a notebook binder that provides usage information for equipment such as the phone or DVD player and recommendations for local activities and restaurants. Orient yourself using the resort map. Look for emergency exits and fire extinguishers. Some resorts now have defibrillators scattered around the resort. Find out where these are located as well as where to take your trash since it may not be emptied for you during your week. Many resorts have centrally located recycling bins.

Familiarize yourself with the resort's neighborhood. Learn the location of nearby grocery stores from the front desk or information materials, but wait to shop until after check-in just in case you encounter unanticipated delays. You don't want your ice cream to melt while you wait for housekeeping to finish cleaning your unit. Check the local weather and select some restaurants in the local guide. Resorts often provide orientation meetings early in the week to help guests learn about the resort's activities and the local area. Once you understand your options, discuss the week's plans with everyone staying with you.

Avoiding Sales Presentations

Resorts in active developer sales or those affiliated with a vacation club or other related properties, may invite you to a meeting or other veiled sales presentation during your stay. Ask about owners updates or orientation meetings before you agree to attend these presentations. Even if you're staying in the unit through an exchange or rental arrangement, you're under no obligation to attend any sales presentations. However, some people stay in timeshares as part of an incentive package in which they agree to participate in a tour or presentation, so they obviously need to fulfill their obligation.

If you're not obligated and sales people don't take "no" for an answer, unplug the phone or schedule a meeting that you don't intend to keep for the final day so that they'll leave you alone. Larger resorts may also pester you about buying additional services such as photos, paid activities, and spa use throughout your visit.

Enjoying Your Stay

Once you've moved in and learned about your options,  prepare to enjoy your prepaid stay. Get your money's worth and exercise your rights as an owner. Take pleasure in your unit, the resort, and the local area.

Enjoying Your Unit

Opportunities abound to enjoy your unit. Many timeshare owners especially enjoy the entertainment center and cooking. Report any maintenance issues promptly and have realistic expectations regarding the level of service.

Most timeshare units are equipped with DVD players. Rent some DVDs or bring some from home. Buy a local TV Guide when you make your grocery run or access local TV guides on the Internet or with a smart phone application.

The fully equipped kitchen found in larger units provides one of the favorite timeshare features of many cost conscious vacationers. Cooking in your unit saves you money compared to taking a group out to a restaurant in a resort area. Double-check to see what's provided in the kitchen before you go shopping. Not only will using the kitchen save money, but fixing special recipes helps create lasting memories.

Bring any maintenance or housekeeping issues to the attention of the front desk immediately. Unlike wine, maintenance problems do not get better with age. By reporting the problem early, you make it clear that you did not cause the problem and it makes it easier for the staff to relocate you to a different unit if you have not yet unpacked. Make a record of the time you reported the problem, who you talked to, and how you contacted the staff. Do not expect hotel-style resolutions to problems to keep you happy. Timeshares don't typically compensate guests for problems the way that a hotel might, so focus on resolving the issue rather than trying to get rewarded for your inconvenience.

A timeshare vacation differs from a hotel stay. The experience is tailored toward people who spend more time at the resort and in their unit and stay for a longer period of time. Remember, this is more like renting a furnished apartment for a week than staying at a hotel for seven nights. Unlike hotels that provide daily maid service, a timeshare resort's housekeeping staff normally cleans units only when the occupants change (typically once a week). However, many timeshare resorts provide a complimentary mid week tidy service where they take out the trash and change the linens. They may also provide additional cleanings for a fee. Unlike a hotel, most timeshare resorts don't deliver fresh towels to your unit and the pool area each day. Instead, they typically leave a set of pool towels in the unit to use throughout your stay. Some resorts have free towel exchanges in their laundry area. Alternatively, you can launder your own towels if your unit has a washer and dryer or if there are common laundry facilities available.

Enjoying Your Resort

Enjoy your time at the resort by using the amenities and participating in the activities. Many timeshare owners discover a favorite area of the resort and fall into a familiar routine each visit. The familiarity and memories of prior visits can be comforting and stress relieving.

At check-in, you may be provided with an activities calendar. Study these materials to learn about available activities and resort amenities. Some activities may be restricted to kids or adults. Check the local weather and the resort's activity schedule to plan your week. Highlight the activities schedule to organize your plans.

The resort may charge a small fee for participation in some activities. Activities offer an opportunity to meet fellow vacationers and make new friends. Take pictures of friends and family enjoying the activities and amenities because your timeshare experience creates opportunities for making lifelong memories.

Keep in mind that your actions impact maintenance costs. For example, leaving the air conditioning on when you leave the unit adds to the resort's electric bill which affects your maintenance fee costs as an owner. Help minimize the resort's laundry costs by reusing towels. Remember, you're not only a guest – you're an owner who pays for your share of repairs and upkeep.

Enjoying the Local Area

You probably selected the timeshare based largely on its location. Each destination has its own unique attractions, shops, and restaurants to explore. Some resorts organize excursions to local attractions. Find local libraries and movie theaters. Some timeshare owners request a local library card by showing evidence of the property tax payment that's included in their timeshare maintenance fees.

> "All good things must come to an end."
>
> --based on an English proverb by Chaucer ~1374

Departing

Leaving the resort requires preparing for your departure, checking out with the front desk, and reporting on your stay.

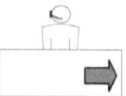

Preparing for Departure

Be aware of the posted checkout deadline, normally around 10 a.m. or 11 a.m. Leave plenty of time to prepare for the checkout process. There's usually not much time between your departure and the next guest checking in, so it's important to leave on time. The resort may fine you if you stay past checkout time. Start packing in the kitchen since you may need time for the dishwasher to run through its cycles. Don't forget to look in the refrigerator for dishes that belong to the resort and need to be cleaned before you leave. Take out the garbage last. The resort often suggests a recommended tip amount for the cleaning staff. Take into consideration the number of times the unit was cleaned during the week and the fact that the unit is much larger than a standard hotel room.

Checking Out

At the end of your timeshare stay, you typically check out in a process similar to that of a hotel. The process may be as simple as returning the keys and pool bracelets or it may involve reviewing and settling the account for incidentals. Return your keys before the checkout deadline and let the front desk know that you're leaving so that they can begin to clean the unit.

Compared to many hotel stays that result in unexpected charges like resort fees and high taxes, it's a nice feeling to check out without receiving a bill. But, although you've already paid your annual maintenance fees plus the original cost of the timeshare, don't expect to escape without any extra costs. If you've charged anything to your unit such as drinks at the bar, you must settle those charges when you leave.

If you're a floating week owner, and you must be within a twelve month window to make a reservation, consider making your reservation for the following year's use as you check out. However, keep in mind that some timeshares prohibit floating week owners from using their week over the same federal holiday two years in a row.

If you have a late flight, or aren't ready to leave, the resort may allow you to continue using common areas throughout the rest of the departure day. You might also arrange to rent an extra day or two before or after your stay.

Providing Feedback and Reporting on Your Stay

When you go to the office to check out, be sure to point out any unresolved maintenance issues and provide feedback on your stay. If any employees helped make your stay especially memorable, be sure to identify them to the people at the front desk.

Resort managers should welcome your opinions as a way to improve the experience for future guests. Well-managed resorts provide survey forms because they recognize the value of guest feedback. Surveys communicate your concerns and opinions to management and should be carefully read by the management team. Actions for resolving issues should be carefully tracked. If you feel like your recommendations are not being acted on by the management, consider escalating your concerns by communicating directly with the HOA.

Reviews provide recent information that helps people considering buying or staying at the resort. Consider writing a review for a timeshare magazine or travel website to share your experience with others. Upload your pictures to websites like Facebook to share them with others. Pictures that you upload with online reviews help others learn more about the resort without having to physically travel there. Sharing your experiences with friends also advertises your timeshare, a benefit when it comes time to rent or sell it.

Extending Use and Involvement Throughout the Year

Owning a timeshare involves more than merely enjoying your one week a year at the resort. You may be able to access the resort at other times during the year if you have day use benefits or bonus time access. Stay in communication with the resort throughout the year and participate in the broader community of timeshare owners. Also, continue to learn about timeshares.

Day Use Privileges

If your ownership entitles you to day use privileges, you can enjoy some of the resort's amenities like the pool even when you're not staying overnight at the resort. Understanding the rules for day use privileges ensures a successful extension of your timeshare use. Some timeshares restrict the number of owners who can access their day use benefits on a particular day or restrict access to certain amenities. For example, the number of owners that can use their day use privileges may be limited on a first-come first-served basis. Some local owners use day use privileges like a country club membership.

Certain resorts limit day use benefits to owners that buy directly from the developer and don't allow those benefits to convey to resale purchasers. Access to a nearby timeshare on the beach certainly beats using a public park's facilities.

Bonus Time

As an owner at some timeshares, you may have access to bonus time programs. This is usually a discounted rental program using unused or foreclosed weeks controlled by the HOA. This benefit allows you to stay at your resort more than once a year at a discounted cost. Typically, an owner (someone named on the deed) must accompany the group accessing bonus time or day use benefits.

Staying Involved

Stay involved with your timeshare even after you've checked out by staying in communication with the resort, and possibly participating in the HOA. Stay current on resort news by reading the resort's newsletters and other posted information on the resort's website.

Your timeshare may be managed by a HOA that is led by a BoD. If your resort has a HOA, exercise your right to vote for directors when you receive a ballot. Consider volunteering to serve on the board. This is typically a thankless job, but provides fascinating insights into how the resort operates and how decisions are made.

Attend HOA meetings to voice your suggestions and concerns. If you can't attend HOA meetings, vote your proxy to help meet quorum requirements and avoid unnecessary expenses associated with rescheduling meetings and collecting votes. Access and read HOA meeting minutes from the resort's website if available.

Participating in the Timeshare Community

Consider participating in online message forums to contribute to the community of fellow timeshare owners. This enables you to pass on your lessons learned and perspectives to help fellow owners. However, remember that online communities often attract content contributors with questionable motives and conflicts of interest.

The premier online community for timeshare owners is the Timeshare User's Group (TUG). Bill Rogers formed the TUG after a bad exchange experience and grew it into the premier site for timeshare-related information. TUG provides advice articles, resort reviews, and message forums. TUG message forums are read by more than 50,000 registered users.

TUG members support the forums by submitting answers to posted questions. Many TUG participants graciously share their sage advice and helpful perspectives. They offer invaluable advice based on their rich set of knowledge and experiences.

Initially, the advice on TUG was more focused on questions regarding individual resorts and destinations, but has grown to cover every aspect of timesharing. Although online message forums are moderated, there's no guarantee that contributors are offering accurate and unbiased information. Moderators and participants usually do a good job of correcting inaccuracies and squelching misleading postings. Get answers for your legal and tax questions from professionals and don't hesitate to get a second opinion from helpful organizations such as the NTOA.

Consider visiting and joining TUG even if you don't yet own a timeshare. TUG membership fees in 2011 were only $15 per year and multi-year memberships receive discounts. Members can access restricted content and can place advertisements on the website for free.

Another popular online community for timeshare owners is TimeshareForums. The TimeshareForums website has many of the same features as TUG's Timeshare Community Forums (called TUG BBS).

Continued Education

Try and validate that timeshare information you receive is based on authoritative sources. Consider participating in owners associations. A Maryland timeshare owners group helped form the National Timeshare Owners Association (NTOA). Guest speakers at NTOA meetings share travel recommendations with members who discuss pointers with each other. The NTOA provides advice and consumer protection by forwarding information from sources such as state Attorneys General offices, the real estate commission of the state where the contract is written, the Federal Trade Commission (FTC), and the Better Business Bureau (BBB).

A number of books have been written about timeshares, and a list of the best ones is available on the companion website. Consider subscribing to one of the magazines or newsletters devoted to timeshare owners. *TimeSharing Today* provides a wealth of useful information and has helped organize owners groups. The *Owners Perspective* magazine is another useful resource. Reading books and magazines intended for timeshare developers and sales people provides an interesting behind the scenes perspective on the industry.

Alternatives to Using Your Week Yourself

If you can't use your week yourself, it doesn't have to go unused. If you own points, you may be able to roll them over to the next year or transfer them to someone else for a fee. If you're unable to use your week yourself, consider allowing friends or family to use it. You can always exchange it or try and rent it out. If you own a deeded timeshare, you might be able to convert it into a points membership that would provide you more flexibility. If you're finding that you rarely use your unit yourself, consider disposing of it (see Chapter 6).

Some people waste their week by allowing it to go unused. Maintenance fees must be paid even if no one uses the unit. If you don't use, rent, or exchange your week, it may remain empty. What a waste! If you're feeling generous, consider letting friends or family use your week. Share unused days with them if you can't stay all seven days. If you're unable or uninterested in using your week a particular year, this approach is a fairly simple way to get some value out of the week. Letting a friend or relative use your week is similar to renting the week for free. However, you may have to pay for a guest certificate at some vacation clubs.

Exchanging involves transferring your right to use your week to gain the use of someone else's week. There is no guarantee that you'll get the exchange you want and exchanging usually requires additional fees. Chapter 4 provides suggestions on exchanging your week. Unless your plans change within a couple of weeks of your reservation date, plan on banking your week with an exchange company.

Although renting out your unit would intuitively seem to be a profitable use of your week, it's often difficult to find renters unless you have a high demand week in a popular destination. If you are able to rent your week, the rent will rarely cover your annual maintenance fee costs. Chapter 5 provides suggestions on renting out your unit.

If you enjoy timesharing, but find yourself exchanging your deeded timeshare most of the time, consider converting your deeded timeshare to a points system. Be careful not to pay too much for the conversion. Many companies have learned that selling points conversions produces significant revenues. Although some sales techniques suggest that you must convert when the resort begins selling points, if you already have a deeded week you are not required to convert. You still own your deeded week.

If you're interested in owning a points membership, think about buying a resale timeshare that already uses points instead of paying a conversion fee. As with all timeshare decisions, take your time, educate yourself on the options, the advantages and disadvantages, and then make an informed choice.

In the long term, it only makes sense financially to plan on using your timeshare yourself. If you find that you're not using your timeshare on a regular basis, it may be time to consider disposing of it. Chapter 6 provides information on disposing of a timeshare.

Timeshare Use Summary

The whole reason to buy a timeshare is to use it. Maximize your enjoyment of your week by planning ahead. In most cases, if you can't use your week, you can exchange it or rent it out. If you find that you're not using it on a regular basis, think about disposing of it.

You can exchange your right to access your week at your resort during a particular year to instead access a unit at someone else's resort. Exchanging gives you the opportunity to travel to different places. It also allows you to use resorts that would be expensive to rent. By exercising this option, you're not permanently trading away your week.

A popular misconception is that you must use your week each year at the same time at the same location. Some timeshare ownerships provide the flexibility to use other resorts within a group of affiliated resorts and most timeshare resorts are affiliated with companies that facilitate exchanges. For example, if you own a week in Orlando you might decide that you want to vacation in Cancun instead next year. If someone in Cancun is also interested in exchanging their week, you may be able to give up access to your week in order to use their week instead.

Exchanging is a useful timeshare feature that provides opportunities for exploring other destinations. However, many owners experience disappointment when they attempt to perform an exchange because they do not fully understand how to effectively perform the transaction. Avoid frustration by having realistic expectations that are based on the exchange value of the week you're trading.

Why Would You Want to Exchange?

Why exchange your dream timeshare for one somewhere else? The reasons for exchanging range from practical to indulging. Some owners exchange their timeshare as an alternative to a hotel stay, for a business trip, or to attend an event. Exchanging provides flexibility in the timeframe and location of a timeshare stay. Some owners want to try a timeshare in a new location for variety. Fixed week owners may want to exchange in order to travel at a different time of the year than the week that they own. Exchanging is an excellent way to preview another timeshare you're considering buying or renting. Some people deposit their week with an exchange company to obtain bonus weeks or to obtain two weeks of use out of their lock-off unit. A fortunate few owners skillfully navigate the exchange process to uptrade for a timeshare with a better location, higher quality, or preferred amenities.

You can enjoy a different timeshare for little or possibly no additional cost. Everyone wants to receive a fair trade, but many people look to uptrade. By leveraging the rules of the exchange system, owners trade up or obtain more time. Trading up is possible because some weeks, especially last minute deposits and ones that must be used within the next few weeks, are made available to everyone, even people exchanging an inferior week. Some people make a hobby out of trolling exchange company websites looking for valuable uptrades.

> "The grass is always greener at someone else's timeshare."

Exchange Options

If you want to exchange your timeshare, you have several options including direct exchange, internal exchange, and company-assisted exchange.

Direct Exchange

As the owner of your week, you typically have the right to designate who will use your unit. This privilege, called assignment, allows you to arrange a private exchange with someone else. With this approach, you agree to swap your week directly for a week owned by someone else and you both inform your home resorts that the other person will be using your week. A direct exchange is similar to renting your week to someone who pays you with their week rather than cash.

The biggest advantage of a direct exchange is that you're cutting out the exchange company middlemen and therefore you don't pay exchange fees to anyone. A direct exchange represents the simplest form of exchange to perform, once the two parties find each other and agree on terms.

However, it's difficult to arrange for two owners who want to trade units. That's the biggest disadvantage of a direct exchange, you have to find someone willing to exchange their week for exactly the week that you're offering. Additionally, you might be liable for damages caused by the person using your direct exchange, much like a renter.

Internal Exchange

Some resorts participate in a portfolio of affiliated properties that have their own internal trading program. Resorts in the group often have the same management company. With this option, you trade your week for a week at one of the participating resorts. Although you're limited to exchanges within a small number of resorts, the fees may be less than those charged by independent exchange companies. Rules for internal exchange programs vary widely and information on the program should be available from your resort.

Exchange Company Assisted Exchange

Most people perform timeshare exchanges with the help of companies that specialize in assisting owners find a fair replacement for the use of their week. Exchange companies help developers sell more units by providing flexibility to buyers. Exchange companies make their money from exchange fees, annual membership dues, and renting unused units. Exchange companies maintain a large inventory of weeks offered for exchange, called banked or deposited weeks. They provide weeks to owners in exchange for depositing comparable accommodations. Because of the domino effect characteristic of exchanges, you don't have to wait for someone to withdraw your week for you to obtain a week from the inventory.

Determining Exchange Value

To perform an equitable trade you need to know the value of the item being exchanged. Some people call a week with a high exchange value a "tiger trader". A week's exchange value also affects its purchase price because timeshare weeks with high exchange value are more desirable. Some buyers actively hunt for tiger traders with low annual maintenance fees that they intend to only use for exchange purposes.

One approach for determining equitable exchanges is to use a points-based system. A points-based exchange system provides transparency so you know the exact exchange value of your week and the value of the week you're exchanging into.

Exchange values are based primarily upon supply and demand. Unfortunately, exchange companies have historically limited access to the valuing formulas they use. However, based on explanations from the companies and personal experience, several supply and demand factors affecting exchange values for timeshares have been identified and are shown in Table 8.

Table 8. Exchange Value Factors

Factor	Affects Supply	Affects Demand
Perceived quality and reputation		X
Season / week of year	X	X
Popularity/desirability of location	X	X
Respected / well-known brand name		X
Number of built units in a particular area	X	
Timing (how early it's deposited)	X	
Ease of travel access		X

An exchanged week receives its value at the time of deposit – the point when the owner gives up their right to their week. Once you deposit a week, the exchange value is locked in. Therefore, you don't have to worry about the exchange value deflating as the check-in date approaches while you wait to select or obtain the target week for your exchange.

Exchange value is sometimes difficult to predict. You may get a better sense once you deposit your week and you begin to see the options you're offered. Demand for some resorts varies week by week. Contiguous weeks may be grouped into seasons. The printed II directory provides an indication of relative demand by week for resorts in a region. Similarly, the RCI Weeks website provides an indication of demand through its exchange planner feature. Resort week demand may also be tiered for points systems and internal exchange programs. Season colors may indicate relative value at a particular resort, but can't be used reliably to compare with weeks at other resorts. Quality tiers help describe the relative condition of a resort. However, these are not indicators of demand or exchange value.

Timing

One major factor affecting exchange value is the timeliness of the deposit. Depositing adds your week to the exchange company's available inventory. That transaction may satisfy someone else's ongoing search. Exchange companies assign a higher exchange value to deposits made a year or more ahead of their use date. They credit early deposits with higher exchange values to build up their available inventory. Also, by having a week available longer, the exchange company has a better chance of finding someone that wants the week and is willing to pay the exchange fee. Conversely, last minute deposits receive a penalty through lower exchange values. Some exchange companies relax quality restrictions close to the use date. Therefore, they may provide a high quality week available close to check-in time for a low quality week deposited early. Some people score great exchanges with low quality weeks by depositing early and submitting on-going requests.

If you cancel an exchange, you may regain credit for the week you originally deposited and used to make the cancelled exchange. This is called a redeposit. Redeposited weeks may have less value or time restrictions.

Realistic Expectations Based on Exchange Value

Recognize the relative exchange value of your week so that you won't be disappointed with the exchange offers you receive. Once you have a feel for the exchange value of the week you're trading, expect equitable trade options.

One way to determine exchange value is to get points-based offers from companies that perform exchanges using that approach. Then compare the points offered to the points required for desired exchanges. For example, if a points-based exchange system offers you thirty exchange points for your Christmas week in Orlando, shop their website to see what you could get for those thirty points. RCI has a deposit calculator on their website that provides members with potential deposit values. Another method is to compare offered exchange weeks (after you've deposited) to weeks available for rent. Hopefully, you'll be offered weeks that rent for more than the maintenance fees of the week you deposited.

Affiliated Exchange Companies

Most resorts and RTU systems partner with one or more exchange companies by signing agreements that provide owners with access to the affiliated exchange company's services. Working with an affiliated company simplifies the exchange process because your resort has an established relationship with the exchange company. Resorts participating in an affiliation agreement are listed in the affiliated exchange company's catalog of resorts. An affiliated exchange company may be initially selected by the developer, but then eventually changed by the HOA that takes over control. The company managing an RTU system, such as a vacation club, selects the affiliated exchange company.

RCI and II are the two largest affiliated exchange companies. Most resorts partner with one or both of these companies. Ask your resort if they have an affiliation agreement in place or look at the directory of resorts on the exchange company's website.

Because the affiliated exchange company already enjoys a relationship with the resort, using it simplifies any exchange transaction that occurs. Additionally, the affiliation agreement protects the owner from liability for damages caused by exchangers who access the week through the affiliated exchange company. By being a member with an affiliated exchange company, you may become eligible to rent the exchange company's unused weeks.

The primary disadvantage of using an affiliated exchange company, however, lies in the annual membership dues and exchange-related fees. Exchange companies vary in the fees they charge such as initiation fees, annual membership fees, exchange fees, and guest fees. They also differ in the services they offer. Some developers provide membership to the affiliated exchange company when you buy from them. However, this perk isn't worth the difference in price over buying resale.

RCI is the largest timeshare exchange company. Its exchange program, now called RCI Weeks, was started in 1974. As of 2011, RCI was part of Wyndham Worldwide Corporation. Some members have an issue with RCI renting out deposited weeks, and making weeks available to members of the points system called RCI Points, because they believe it makes it harder to find a week to obtain for an exchange. Members receive an RCI magazine and may be offered an RCI-branded credit card.

Interval International (II) began supporting exchanges in 1976. As of 2011, it was part of the Interval Leisure Group. II members own weeks or points at II-affiliated resorts. II's system primarily supports exchanges. However, they also rent unused weeks to members through their Getaway program and provide discounts on rental cars, cruises, and vacation packages. II members are also offered credit cards. Guest certificates allow others, if you cannot accompany them, to use your exchange or Getaway. II also provides a full service travel agency, online services, and a members-only travel magazine.

II charges an annual membership fee. However, they sometimes waive this fee as part of a developer-based purchase. II has different membership levels with slightly different benefits. II's higher tiers of membership, called Interval Gold and Interval Platinum, benefit frequent purchasers of their rentals because of discounts provided with those membership types. Be sure to read and understand the terms and conditions of membership on the company's website before joining.

One advantage of using an affiliated exchange company is that they guarantee to accept any deposited week from an affiliated resort. A non-affiliated company might turn away the exchange if they perceive that the week has a low exchange value. The two large exchange companies have more resorts available for potential exchange than other exchange companies. Another advantage of using an affiliated exchange company is that you will not be held liable for damages caused by people using an exchange facilitated by an affiliated company.

Both RCI and II have a large number of affiliated resorts and maintain a large inventory of weeks available for exchange. Few resorts affiliate with both of the major exchange companies, so it's rare to have to pick between which of the two companies to join. Table 9 contrasts the two major exchange companies and their fees as of 2011.

Table 9. Contrasting the Two Major Exchange Companies

Company	RCI	Interval International (II)
Year Started	1974	1976
Number of members	About 3.8M	About 1.9M
Annual Fee	$89	$89
Exchange Fee	$194 (domestic and international) $15 discount for online transactions ($179)	$159 (same country as member) $174 (different country than member) $20 discount for online transactions
Bonus Weeks	Extra Vacations	Accommodation Certificates
Affiliation Required	Yes	Yes
Number of resorts	Over 3,700	Over 2,500
Major Vacation Club Affiliations	Disney, Hilton (primary)	Marriott, Hyatt, Starwood (primary)
Countries	About 100	Over 75
Deposit Extension	$69 for 3 months $109 for 6 months	$59 for 3 months $89 for 6 months $169 for 12 months
Guest Certificate	$59	$49
Magazine	Endless Vacation Magazine	Interval World Magazine
Credit Card	RCI Elite Rewards World MasterCard	Interval International Visa Signature card
Rental Program	Extra Vacations and Last Call	Getaways
Higher Membership Tiers	Platinum	Gold, Platinum

Unaffiliated Exchange Companies

RCI and II perform the vast majority of timeshare exchanges. However, other smaller exchange companies exist. Although in some rare cases, these companies may be formally affiliated with a resort, they're typically referred to as unaffiliated exchange companies. These alternative exchange companies provide services with some advantages over the two large companies. However, their inventory is much more limited.

Platinum Interchange, Dial an Exchange, and Trading Places International are three of the unaffiliated exchange companies. Trading Places International was purchased in 2010 by II's parent organization, but is operated independently. Some of the exchange companies collaborate with each other in the Cooperative Association of Resort Exchangers (C.A.R.E), a timeshare trade association that focuses on helping their member companies exchange, rent, and manage their inventories of available weeks.

Because these companies have a smaller inventory to offer, they work hard to provide compensating features. Unaffiliated companies may have lower costs including no membership fees and lower exchange fees. Smaller exchange companies also try to provide better customer service as they work diligently to compete with the large companies for your business. You may want to consider an unaffiliated company if you're interested in exchanging into a particular region. For example, Dial an Exchange may be your best bet if you're trying to go to Australia, which is where they're based.

With unaffiliated companies, the resort may treat the exchange as if you are having a friend or relative use your unit or as if you rented it out yourself. If you use an unaffiliated exchange company, you might be liable for damages caused by the people that use your week. The primary disadvantage lies in the fact that that independent exchange companies maintain much smaller inventories of available weeks than RCI and II.

Choosing an Exchange Option

Although direct exchanges occasionally occur, most timeshare owners use an exchange company. Exchange company websites list their rules. However, it's often difficult to determine how some of the trading companies actually value weeks and how they decide whether to rent or make weeks available for exchanges. Points-based exchange systems are more transparent. *TimeSharing Today* periodically publishes a very useful comparison of exchange companies. Table 10 summarizes the exchange options.

Table 10. Exchange Option Summary

Exchange Option	Advantages	Disadvantages
Direct Exchange	No cost to either exchanger	Difficult to find another exchanger
Internal Exchange	Lower cost than using an exchange company	Less inventory than affiliated companies
Affiliated Exchange Company	Large inventory and easy to work with your resort	Higher exchange cost and annual membership cost
Unaffiliated Exchange Company	Lower cost than affiliated companies	Less inventory than affiliated companies

Direct Exchange Process

Performing direct exchanges involves securing your week, finding another week available for direct exchange, performing the exchange, including all necessary documentation and notifications, and using the unit.

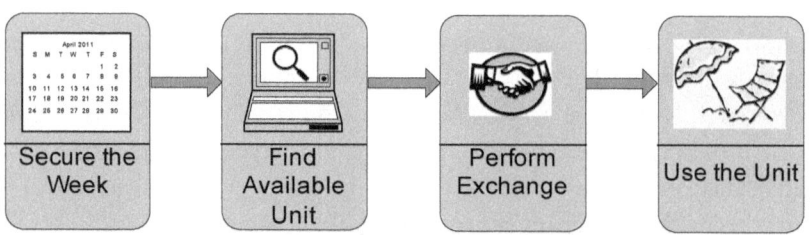

Figure 12. Direct Exchange Process

Securing the Week

Before you exchange your week, unless you have a fixed week, make sure you have a week reserved with your resort. If you've already been communicating with a potential direct exchanger, you can try and reserve their preferred week.

Otherwise, reserve a valuable week that will be popular with potential exchangers. Find out if there's a fee for changing the reservation date in case the person that you're exchanging with decides they want a different week than the one you've reserved.

Finding an Available Week

Finding a week available for a direct exchange requires locating an owner who is interested in performing a direct exchange and has a week you'd be interested in using. TUG has a forum on their website to help owners interested in direct exchanges find each other. Search listings of offered exchanges. If you don't find one, post your interest. Include what you have to offer, what you are looking for, and your contact information.

Performing the Direct Exchange

Once you find someone to exchange with and agree to participate in the exchange, document the agreement in an email or letter that specifies what happens if either party wants to cancel the arrangement. Once the document is agreed to by both parties, each owner should inform their respective resorts that someone else will be using their unit and provide the resort with the contact information of the other party. Notify your resorts within an agreed upon number of days and obtain reservation confirmations for the assigned users. Agree to assume responsibility for your own damages.

Using the Unit

The exchange guest should receive the same rights and privileges as someone using the unit for free as a guest of the owner. The person using your week may be required to provide a security deposit. Follow up with the other owner and stay in touch in case you want to repeat the direct exchange in the future.

Assisted Exchange Process

The assisted exchange process varies depending on whether you commit to depositing your week or only make an exchange request contingent upon a desirable choice becoming available. The exchange process is summarized in Figure 13.

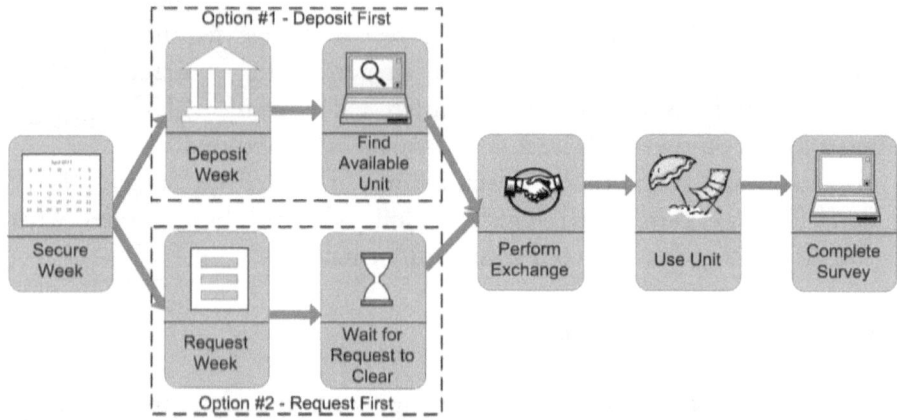

Figure 13. Assisted Exchange Process

Each exchange company has very specific rules and processes for performing an exchange with their company's help. Look in the resort directory or on their website to learn how they operate. The process can be complex and very confusing the first time you perform an exchange. The biggest decision affecting your exchange process may be deciding whether you want to deposit a week before searching (option #1) or make a contingent exchange based on a desired exchange becoming available (option #2).

Securing Your Week for an Assisted Exchange

You must have something tangible to trade (your week) in order to obtain someone else's week. You may need to pay your maintenance fees before you can secure your week for exchanging.

If you own a floating week or points, reserve a specific week to offer in exchange. Usually, you follow a similar process as you do when reserving your week for your own use. Of course, if you have a fixed week, you skip this step because you already know that you have a reserved week. If you own a floating week, reserve a week that will be valued by the exchange company.

Lock-off owners must decide in advance how best to configure their unit for exchange. Owners often split lock-off units and use or exchange the subunits separately. This creates an opportunity to access two weeks instead of one. If you own a high value lock-off week, the exchange company may allow you to deposit the smaller efficiency side in addition to the main part of the unit.

The next step in the process depends on whether you want to deposit first (Option #1) or request first (Option #2). The primary factors impacting the option you select are whether your check-in date is approaching soon and whether you already know where you'd like to go.

Depositing Your Week with the Exchange Company (Option #1)

If you're nearing your check-in date, won't be able to use your week, and don't have firm plans for a future vacation, you may want to deposit your week with an exchange company. The specific process depends on which exchange company you  use. Call the exchange company or go to their website for more details. Ask your resort whether to contact their office or the exchange company to make the deposit. If you contact the exchange company to make the deposit, they'll verify the week with the resort. Sometimes, there are advantages in working through your resort to deposit your week. For example, if you're performing a deposit close to the check-in date, the resort may be able to move your reservation to a later date before they deposit it, so that it won't be considered a last minute deposit with low value.

Deposit your week as early as possible. Exchange companies claim that early deposits improve your odds of receiving a requested week. To maximize your exchange value, deposit at least a year ahead of time.

If you have a very desirable week available for deposit, the exchange company may offer you a bonus week as an incentive for depositing it. For example, II sometimes provides bonus week coupons called accommodation certificates when you deposit a high demand week. However, it's difficult to determine which weeks are eligible for these rewards without initiating the deposit process. The bonus week may provide you an additional week of timeshare use, but it may also come with several restrictions. You'll be charged an exchange fee when you use a bonus week, so these coupons may not be as valuable as first perceived.

Exchange companies limit the time you have available to use a deposited week, although they may allow you to pay a fee to extend the deposited week's expiration date. There are also limits on how early you can deposit.

Finding an Available Unit (Option #1)

Once you've deposited a week, look for an available week  that satisfies your exchange criteria. Normally, exchangers select one or more potential destinations before looking for an exchange. However, it's fun to browse all the potential destinations available that you can exchange into. When you find a potential exchange, research the offered resort to determine whether it fits your interests and preferences.

Resort directories educate members about potential exchange options. However, the directories also serve as marketing tools for the exchange companies and may not fully represent the current condition of the described resorts. For example, the pictures in the directory may have been taken years ago. Your success in finding a good exchange depends upon your own flexibility and spontaneity, as well as the demand for the resort and timeframe.

Searching

Begin searching as soon as your deposit has been accepted by the exchange company. Search parameters and criteria include geographic area, minimum unit size, specific resorts, and timeframe. Exchange companies group resorts into geographic regions that range from entire continents such as South America to specific cities such as Las Vegas.

To determine the availability of weeks for trade, call the exchange company or query online using their website. The search process is similar to shopping for an airfare – try several dates and destinations. The exchange assistance person answering phone calls may be able to work the exchange company's computer system best.

Exchange company websites provide multiple search options such as clicking on a map or typing in the location name or resort name. Be flexible with search parameters. Start with your specific desires and then begin relaxing those parameters as you alter acceptable dates and geographic areas. When you enter a request, the exchange company queries their databases to provide you with a list of weeks currently in their inventory that match your search parameters and would provide an equitable exchange for the week you want to exchange. If you like one of the offered exchanges, you can make the exchange immediately. If no equitable exchanges meet your criteria, you might want to enter an on-going search request (described below). As other owners deposit weeks, they may trigger exchanges that match ongoing search requests. Therefore, searches against the currently available inventory may give the false impression that quality exchange options are unavailable because deposited weeks fulfill ongoing requests rather than being added to the inventory.

Equitable Trading

Your goal as an exchanger should be to obtain an equitable trade or an uptrade (if you're lucky). No one wants to feel cheated by trading their valuable week for an inferior week. Determining an equitable trade requires an assessment of the exchange value of your week and the week you're trying to obtain.

The exchange company mandates the value of the units available to you for exchange, and only offer those they deem fair trades. The exchange company's computers will attempt to match exchange value. Results with much lower quality may be omitted so that you aren't disappointed with the exchange. Exchanges into much higher quality units may not be offered if the exchange isn't considered equitable. The RCI Weeks program allows you to combine weeks or residual exchange credits from past exchanges to increase your trading power.

The perceived exchange value of your week depends on several supply and demand factors including location, quality, and amenities. The factors that influence your trading power are encoded into computer software used by the exchange companies. The software uses internal valuation models to determine trading equity. The exchange value of your week is explicit when you use a more transparent system such as RCI Weeks which provides an online deposit calculator. Have a realistic expectation of the value of the week that you're exchanging. The exchange companies' designated quality tiers help indicate superior properties. However, some frequent exchangers question whether some specific properties deserve their ratings.

Selecting a General Destination to Trade Into

Some people begin their search by looking at availability first, and then selecting a destination. Have some fun with the process, however, and enter the widest possible dates and select the option to view all destinations to browse all the possibilities. If you know where you'd like to go, narrow your search by selecting the general geographic area of interest such as Hawaii, Colorado, or Europe. Once you've selected the area, familiarize yourself with the resorts where possible exchanges are located. You'll likely find plenty of choices in areas that have many resorts such as Orlando or the Canary Islands. However, it's usually difficult to find availability in popular areas with few timeshare resorts such as Paris or Boston.

Prepare yourself for plenty of uncertainty and a lack of guarantees. Searching for a timeshare exchange is nothing like searching for a hotel room – it's probably more similar to online dating. Only a fraction of timeshare inventory is available for trades. Remember, timeshares typically sustain a higher occupancy rate than hotels and exchange availability usually results from an owner giving up their week for a potential exchange.

Some weeks in the exchange company inventories come from bulk deposits by resorts. Resorts sometimes deposit several weeks to the exchange company that are owned by the HOA or cannot be used by owners that are delinquent with their maintenance fees. These deposits are made to obtain credits with the exchange company for future use. Resorts pass along the credits to compensate owners that aren't able to access their unit because of major repairs or renovations.

Juding the Quality of Offered Exchanges

Finding an equitable trade is one of the biggest challenges in exchanging timeshares. The exchange should be fair, but often exchangers feel like they have traded down, leading to disappointment. On the other hand, some exchangers are excited to obtain a significant uptrade.

Exchange companies generate revenues by receiving payment for exchanges that result from their efforts. However, they want return business and satisfied customers, so they work hard to facilitate equitable trades. Determining exchange equity requires placing a value on the weeks in a fairly objective manner. A variety of factors affect the value of a trade just as happens with purchasing a unit. Again, these factors include season, size of unit, view, and location. Have realistic expectations of your week's exchange value. If you have a floating week, experiment with various available check-in dates to maximize the trading power value the exchange companies offer.

The exchange companies' quality tiers may help you judge the quality of the resort they're offering. However, don't rely on an exchange company's description of an available resort. The exchange companies publish catalogs and website listings that describe participating resorts in their networks. However, these descriptions may be dated. Just as with buying, look at reviews before agreeing to an exchange. There's no substitute for firsthand experience gained from staying at or touring a resort.

The desirability of a particular calendar week varies widely. Color coding sometimes provides a basis of comparison. Historically, companies used the color red to identify the highest demand weeks. However, refrain from using color codes to compare resorts with each other. II publishes a chart that shows the popularity of certain locations during each week of the year. Based on local hotel data, their chart indicates potential demand. Similarly, RCI provides an online exchange planner that indicates the typical availability of certain weeks of the year within a particular region.

To protect you from disappointment, the exchange company tries to offer you trades that do not represent a significant downgrade in quality. This is sometimes called a quality filter. However, if you want to know about all possible exchanges, speak with one of the exchange company's representatives. Some people believe that the customer service agents can manually override that setting in their software.

Improving Your Odds

Check the exchange company's website or call often to determine what units are available for an uptrade. The exchange company's inventory changes constantly as people make deposits and exchanges. Successful uptrading requires patience, luck, flexibility, and persistence.

Some people make a hobby out of looking for uptrade opportunities and sharing their finds with others looking for good exchanges. The Timeshare User's Group (TUG) website includes a "Sightings/Distressed" forum where members list valuable weeks that members have discovered are available for exchange.

The biggest opportunity to trade up comes from exchanging into a week with a limited amount of time remaining before the check-in date.

The exchange companies make money by exchanging or renting a week in their inventory before the check-in date. As the check-in date approaches, the opportunity to profit from an exchange fee declines. Therefore, exchange companies sometimes relax equitable trade restrictions during the last couple of months before the check-in date to increase the odds of obtaining an exchange fee.

II has a "Flex Exchange" system for weeks with a check-in date within the next two months. RCI uses a similar process that it calls "Last Call". When the exchange company makes more inventory available at the last minute, your ability to trade up may increase significantly.

Exchange companies may also try to rent weeks they've been unable to exchange. When you perform an exchange, you're effectively renting a week and using your week and the exchange fees as payment. Therefore, always compare the requested rental amount to the sum of your annual maintenance fees and the exchange fee.

Sometimes, it makes more sense to rent instead of exchange. Since renting doesn't require you to forfeit the use of you week, you might want to rent the offered week and keep your week instead of performing an exchange.

One downside of a last minute trade is that your plane tickets may be expensive because there are fewer cheap airfares available within two months of the departure date. However, if you're using frequent flier miles, you may find that the airline makes additional seats available for award redemptions at the last minute. This is because they are constantly reevaluating their ability to sell the remaining seats on a particular flight. Also, airline employees with flight benefits may be able to take advantage of these last minute exchange opportunities if they anticipate available flights.

Exchange Satisfaction

Everyone wants to feel that they received a fair exchange or an uptrade. By owning a valuable week, you improve your chances for good exchanges. Exchange companies want to provide fair and comparable exchanges to keep their customers happy. Some people believe that they can buy a low quality week with a low annual maintenance fee and easily trade it for a high end week on a regular basis. While this may be possible at times, this should not be a motivation for buying a timeshare week because desirable exchanges may not materialize. Avoid disappointment by avoiding trades into a low quality resort. Instead, only exchange into high quality resorts.

Requesting Another Week (Option #2)

Instead of depositing your week first, you may have the option of starting the process by requesting a week at a desired resort. The deposit of your week is contingent on your request being fulfilled. However, many other people may have the same desires that you do for high demand weeks at popular destinations. Therefore, high demand weeks are rarely immediately available in the inventory database. You'll typically be placed on a waiting list until your requested week is available. Your request may or may not be fulfilled depending on how many people deposit the week that you've requested. Request early to improve your chances of receiving the week you want.

Consider trading into a specific resort based on its reputation or location. If you have to specify multiple options, select two impossible exchanges – such as high end resorts in New York City for New Year's or Vail for Christmas as throwaway options, in addition to the exchange that you really want. In the unlikely event that your undesired choices are offered, you should have an opportunity to cancel.

Waiting for Request Fulfillment (Option #2)

When a request cannot be immediately filled, wait for the exchange company to fulfill your request. As you wait to see whether your request is filled, you may be contacted by the exchange companies with offers of alternate choices. You can change your request before it is filled if your plans change or if you want to relax your constraints to improve the odds of finding an exchange. The exchange company may e-mail you a confirmation when they fill an ongoing exchange. Check your email daily for a confirmation since you may have a limited time window, such as 24 hours, to cancel the fulfilled request.

Performing the Assisted Exchange

Performing the exchange requires paying an exchange fee (if not already paid as part of a request). Complete this transaction online or over the phone. The exchange company will send you a confirmation of your new reservation. Be sure to take a copy of that confirmation with you when you go to the resort to check in.

The exchange company may allow you a short period of time, such as 24 hours following an exchange confirmation, to change your mind without penalty. This may occur when you find a week to exchange for your deposit, or when they fulfill your ongoing request. II holds an exchange for a few minutes to gives you time to confer with others or check travel options before committing to the exchange. After the 24 hour period, if you have trader's remorse, or you can't use the week you received in trade, you may be able to redeposit it with certain restrictions. The rules of the exchange company dictate whether you are given the opportunity to perform a different exchange with the week you deposited.

Using the Unit

Once you've performed the exchange, you can look forward to using the week. Verify your reservation ahead of time. Call ahead to request a unit in a desirable area of the resort or one that's been recently renovated.

Take a copy of the exchange confirmation information with you. You'll have similar, but not identical rights and privileges as an owner. However, you'll be treated more like a renter. Exchangers often feel like they are treated as second class citizens because they do not receive all of the perks that owners receive such as early entry hours at an affiliated theme park. There may be additional fees that you pay as an exchanger to access amenities such as parking even though you may not have used those amenities.

Contact the exchange company with any issues at check-in. Recommendations for getting the most out of your stay are covered in Chapter 3.

Resorts sometimes assign exchangers to less desirable units. This occurs because the resort gives priority to its owners (as it should) and tries to please renters by assigning them to better units to try and get them to return again. At resorts with fixed weeks, exchangers often receive the specific unit that was deposited by its owner.

Completing the Survey

The exchange company may ask you to complete a survey after you've used your exchange week. The survey may be provided with the exchange confirmation. Completing the exchange company survey helps influence ratings by the exchange company. Also, consider writing a review for one of the travel review websites or timeshare magazines. This task takes a few minutes of your time, but provides invaluable information that will help potential exchangers learn about the resort.

Alternatives to Exchanging

In addition to traditional exchanging, exchange companies provide other options. You can let friends or family use the week you received in an exchange. You may be able to extend your deposited week if you haven't had an opportunity to perform an exchange. You can also rent a week from an exchange company.

You can't rent out a week you received from an exchange. Exchange companies such as II and RCI strictly prohibit such activity and doing so jeopardizes your membership and your confirmed exchange. However, feel free to bring friends or relatives with you. If your guests plan to arrive first, be sure to ask about check-in procedures and whether that will require a guest certificate.

If you want to give someone else the ability to use the week you received from the exchange, you may have to pay the exchange company to obtain a guest certificate if you won't be accompanying them. You can give friends or family a guest certificate, but you can't charge them because that would be considered renting.

Your deposit might expire before you have a chance to use it. Ask your exchange company about extending the timeframe availability for making the trade. There is usually a fee for extending the deposit depending on the length of the extension.

Exchange companies rent out excess inventory. Therefore, you may find the week you're looking for is available for rent. If you want to go somewhere else but still retain use of the week you own you can rent a week from an exchange company. Sometimes, you can rent a week for less than the maintenance fees owners pay and avoid their long term commitment. With this option, you can pay cash to obtain the week you want without forfeiting the use of your week. One downside to exchange companies renting out their inventory is that fewer weeks may be available for exchangers.

Exchange Summary

When you exchange, keep in mind that you're giving up access to your week during a particular year. Maintenance fees and an exchange fee must be paid to execute an assisted exchange. Successful exchanging requires realistic expectations. The concept of easy trading is one of the most oversold features of timeshares. It is possible to exchange your lower value week for a highly desired resort during a popular week. However, it isn't likely.

Most people use an affiliated exchange company to perform an assisted exchange. If you deposit first, it's easier to see your options. However, you need to use your deposit before it expires. If you request first, you don't have to keep on checking, but you may not find an acceptable exchange within your constraints.

The keys to successful exchanging involve understanding the value of the week you're exchanging, knowing what you're willing to accept, patience, flexibility, luck, and a sense of adventure. The exchange company will try and facilitate an equitable trade, so have that as your expectation. Exchange companies reward early deposits, so try and deposit at least six months but preferably a year prior to use.

Request early so that you'll be high on the waiting list and have a longer window of opportunity for a week to become available. If you do not use the request approach, check the website often and at different times of the day. When an exchange is available, select a resort that you'll enjoy – one with a great location and high quality amenities.

Chapter 5
Renting Your Timeshare to Someone Else

Around 10% of timeshare occupancy is attributed to renters. As a timeshare owner, you may want to occasionally rent your timeshare to someone else instead of using it yourself.

Why Rent Out Your Week?

You may be unable to use your week during a particular year and you may not have the time in your schedule to use a week that you would receive in exchange for your week. You might be able to cover your maintenance fee costs by charging someone else for the right to use your week. If you own a week, not one that you received from an exchange company, you may have the option to rent it out to another party. Some timeshare salespeople claim that it's easy to rent out your week. Although it's often difficult, consider renting your week if you can't use it or exchange it and it's likely to be in demand by renters.

Renting Options

Renting options include renting it through the resort, renting it with the help of a company, renting it on your own, or renting points.

Renting Through the Resort

The easiest method for renting is to add your week to the resort's rental program and allow them to rent it out for you. This approach eliminates the need to find a renter yourself, but is often expensive because the resort will likely keep a large percentage (typically 30%-40%) of the rent in exchange for their rental services. You also run the risk that the unit will not be rented because there is not enough demand (renters) for the supply of available rental units.

Make sure you understand your resort's rental terms. Know where your week falls in priority compared to developer or HOA-owned weeks. Some resorts split weeks and rent by the night like a hotel. This could affect whether you receive payment for a whole week or just a few nights. The resort may pass on some risks on to you. For example, if a tenant cancels their reservation, you may be stuck without a renter at the last minute. Also, renters may want to change their check-in date. The resort may or may not keep your week associated with a renter that changes dates. Resorts usually don't guarantee that your week will rent. Even if you are lucky enough to successfully rent your week each year to cover your maintenance costs, you nevertheless still lose the use of the money you spent on the initial purchase price and closing costs.

Renting Through a Company

Some companies, including some of the smaller exchange companies, provide assistance with renting your week. If you use a rental assistance company that also offers exchange services, you can easily bank the week with them if they aren't able to rent the week. Like a resort, a rental assistance company charges for the service, either as a flat fee or a percentage of the rent.

Renting on Your Own

Renting your week yourself requires taking on responsibility for finding a tenant, executing a lease, and the potential responsibility of damage caused by a tenant. You can achieve higher profits when you rent yourself because you're not sharing the rent with the resort or a rental assistance company. Also, you'll likely work harder to rent your week than someone else would. However, renting on your own may require a great deal of work for one week's rent.

Challenges associated with renting your week yourself include credibility issues with strangers and the risks of non-payment and damages. Some renters are leery of renting from a stranger instead of a company.

Renting Points

If you are part of a points-based system, you may be able to rent or lease points to someone else who then uses the points to reserve a stay at a participating resort. This option offers much less risk for both parties than renting out a week. The transaction resembles a currency exchange.

Some points systems that allowed owners to rent points directly to others now require owners to work through the points management company to rent points. Of course, the company charges for this service, leading to a smaller return for the renting owner.

With a RTU membership, you only have a finite number of years available to use the resort. Therefore, even if your points rent for more than the cost of maintenance fees, you lose one of your limited number of years of use at the timeshare.

Choosing a Renting Option

Unless you have a lot of time on your hands, let the resort rent your week for you. Table 11 summarizes renting options.

Table 11. Renting Option Summary

Renting Option	Advantages	Disadvantages
Renting through the resort	• Easy to arrange • Tenants likely comfortable with transaction • Familiarity with the resort	• High cost due to resort's commission • May not be motivated • Possibly less than whole week rented
Renting through a company	• May work harder than resort to complete the transaction • Lower cost than resort	• May be deposited into company's exchange program • Company may not be able to answer tenant questions
Renting on your own	• No cost • You'll likely work hard to find a renter.	• Tenants may not like dealing with an individual owner
Renting your points	• Simple transaction	• Loss of year's use

Process for Renting Through the Resort

Some resorts help rent weeks in exchange for a hefty percentage of the rent. The process for renting through the resort involves securing the week, completing paperwork for the resort, and waiting for the resort to find a tenant that uses the resort and pays rent so that the resort can send you the proceeds (see Figure 14).

Figure 14. Process for Renting Through Resort

Securing the Week

If you don't own a fixed week, you'll need to reserve the week that you want the resort to try and rent for you. Talk to the resort to try and identify a high demand week so that your odds of renting are high. Also, ask whether rent amounts vary. Some weeks may rent for higher amounts and may provide you more income.

Completing Paperwork

Expect the resort to provide administrative documents for to sign and return, documenting your decision to rent your week. The forms will also require your tax identification information so that the resort can report their payment to you to the IRS.

Resort Finds Tenants

The best part about renting through the resort is that they find the tenants for you. Renters are usually more comfortable dealing with the resort because the process for them is similar to renting a hotel room. Resorts typically set a standard rent amount to maintain consistency with the other units they're offering for rent.

Tenant Uses Resort

The tenant will use the unit and its amenities as if they were the owner or an exchanger. Some minor differences may occur such as having to provide a credit card for a damage deposit or paying some extra fees that owners don't pay. Check with your resort to make sure that you won't be liable for damages caused by tenants that they find.

Owner Receives Rent and Pays Taxes

Once the tenant has paid the rent and used the week, the resort will send you a check for your portion of the rent. Remember, they keep part of the rent as their fee for helping you. Don't forget to account for your rental income on your taxes. See the section below on handling taxes on rental income.

Process for Renting On Your Own

The process for renting on your own involves securing the week, finding a tenant, documenting the agreement, use of the unit by the tenant, the follow up, and paying any taxes that apply (see Figure 15).

Figure 15. Process for Renting on Your Own

Securing the Week

As with exchanges, reserve a floating week before you start the rental process. If you have a choice, reserve a highly desirable week to increase the odds of receiving a high rent for the unit. Again, a week you rent must be one you own, not one you received from an exchange.

Finding Tenants

Finding tenants is the most difficult part of the process when you're renting the week yourself. One challenge is that few travelers understand this option. Many people are leery of renting a timeshare because they fear they'll have to participate in a high pressure sales presentation.

Before you begin searching for a renter, set the rent amount. Set your rental price lower than the resort's published prices since you are competing with them for tenants. Finding renters presents challenges including dealing with an uninformed tenant population, trust issues, and matching your available week with renter demand. The advantage of using a rental assistance company is that they help find and deal with tenants.

Advertise on websites and in publications that specialize in timeshare rentals. Also, consider advertising on Craigslist, Redweek.com, eBay, and in classified ads. Classified ads in magazines like *TimeSharing Today* provide several excellent advertising options. You can also use eBay for one week rentals. Make sure your advertisement clearly states that the auction is for a one time rental of a unit's use and not the permanent sale of the week. If you're advertising to an audience that's not familiar with the timeshare concept, some experts suggest referring to your unit as a condo or a villa instead of a timeshare. That tactic may avoid a potential tenant's fears of having to participate in a sales presentation.

Once a prospective tenant contacts you, be responsive to their questions and offers. First, try and determine their level of understanding about timeshares. If you're lucky, the renter will have experience renting a timeshare and will know what to expect. If not, educate them on timeshares and the differences between timeshares and hotels. Reassure them that they're under no obligation to participate in any tours or sales presentations.

Documenting and Communicating Agreement

Document your agreement with the tenant in a lease. Include names and contact information for both parties and state the terms including check-in/check-out times, security deposit, and payment and cancellation terms. You can obtain sample timeshare rental agreements from online sources. Ask the tenant to send the rent with the signed lease. Reassure hesitant tenants with correspondence from the resort. As a landlord, ask for the rent as early as possible, and definitely before the renters check in. Mandating and receiving a timely payment for the rent helps reduce the risk of non-payment. Also, consider requesting a security deposit since you could be held liable for damages caused by your tenant when they use your week.

Once you have the signed lease and rent payment, provide the name of the renter to the resort. Ask the resort to send a confirmation to the person using the week. This adds to the tenant's comfort level about renting from you.

Tenant Use

Your tenant should receive most of the same privileges that you do when you use your week. Many owners fear the potential liability for damage caused by renters. Ask your resort if you're liable for damages caused by someone using your unit. Resorts typically ask renters for a credit card imprint at check-in as a security deposit. However, some timeshare owners ask their tenants for a security deposit as part of the lease agreement. If you're potentially liable, consider buying renter's insurance to protect yourself from being held responsible for damage caused by your tenant.

Following Up

Contact both the tenant and the resort after the week is used to make sure everything went well. Maintain contact with the tenant in case you want to rent to them again. Ask them how they liked the resort and the unit. Listen to what they liked to help tailor future advertising. Ask them if they mind if you contact them the next time you decide to rent the week. Ask the resort if there were any issues with the tenants.

Paying Taxes

If you're lucky, you might have a few hundred dollars in profit that's subject to taxes. Renting a timeshare creates tax implications similar to renting other types of real estate such as a vacation condo. Although timeshares typically

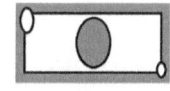

rent for a small amount compared to residential real estate, there may still be a tax liability. In reality, most timeshares rent for little more than the maintenance fees costs. Some states require you to collect sales tax on your rental income.

IRS Regulations

The IRS's vacation home tax rules usually don't apply to rental gains on timeshares since the rental period is short. Report your timeshare rental profits as well as any local sales or occupancy taxes that you owe. IRS regulations document the rules for paying taxes on timeshare rentals. They treat short term rentals of seven days or less differently than long term rentals. Short term rentals do not qualify for declaring rental losses in the same way as other real estate. Consult the detailed section of the income tax regulations (§1.469-1T(e)(3)(ii)) for information on dealing with passive activity losses for vacation rentals of seven days or less.

Determining Profit or Loss

Plan to deduct eligible expenses associated with renting your timeshare as part of reporting timeshare rental income on your taxes. For example, a commission you pay the resort or a rental assistance company can be deducted. To calculate the profit or loss, take the amount collected for rent and subtract deductible expenses.

Rental income is the amount paid by the tenant, not what you receive from the resort or rental assistance company. When you rent out a timeshare, deduct eligible business expenses including advertising, commissions, and maintenance fees associated with renting the week. Most timeshare owners who lose money on their timeshare rentals will only be able to offset passive income such as dividends and interest.

If the resort declares a special assessment for repairs or unexpected expenses, they might be deductible for rentals. You can't deduct special assessments for purposes such as renovations or other major expense covered by the reserve portion of maintenance fees. Additionally, do not deduct the costs associated with traveling to check on your timeshare.

Deducting depreciation is possible, but complicated. To calculate depreciation expense on a rental timeshare, determine the depreciation basis. Depreciation is calculated based on the value when the timeshare became a rental timeshare. If you immediately began using your timeshare for rentals after buying it, then the purchase price you paid is your basis. If you converted your personal timeshare into a rental timeshare, then the resale value at the time of your conversion is the basis. Use the IRS tables to calculate your depreciation expense.

Normally, you can't deduct incurred losses if you rent a unit for a week or less. In this situation, it isn't considered a rental business. IRS rules restrict the treatment of timeshare rental losses as passive. Consider carrying over passive losses against future rental income or deducting them the year you sell the timeshare. Provide your tax accountant with copies of your paid timeshare maintenance fee and special assessment expenses along with information on the rent that you collected.

Renting on Your Own Process Summary

Figure 16 summarizes the process of renting out your week yourself. The specifics may vary but typically include the referenced steps.

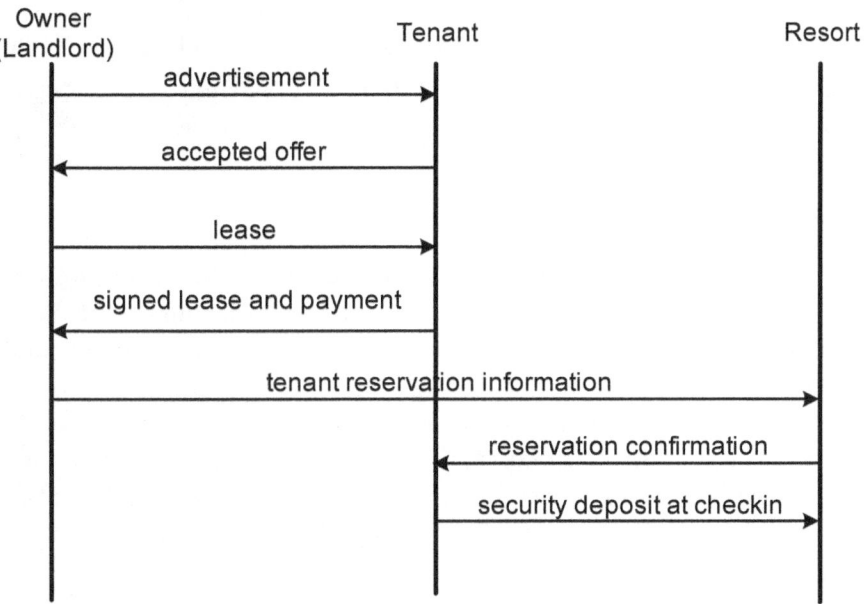

Figure 16. Communication Throughout the Renting Out Process

Alternatives to Renting Out

Since there's no guarantee that your week will rent, always be prepared with a contingency plan. Don't count on the resort notifying you that the week hasn't rented. Put a decision date on your calendar for implementing your backup plan. If you decide not to rent, the tenant backs out, or a tenant isn't found, consider depositing the week with an exchange company, using the week, or donating the week's use to charity.

Calculate deadline dates based on your exchange company's rules for regular and late deposits. Decide whether to wait until the last minute to deposit the week. Some exchange companies accept deposits up to two weeks prior to the check-in date.

If the week doesn't rent, reconsider whether you want to use it. Your schedule may have changed since your decision to try and rent the week. If you still can't enjoy the week yourself, maybe friends or family would appreciate the opportunity to stay there during your week.

In some cases, the resort may rent out less than all seven nights and allow you to use the remaining unrented nights. Consider the option of donating the use of your timeshare week during a particular year. Some charities accept a donation of the use of a timeshare week as an item that they can auction off. While the charity may not receive much for the donation, it's better than letting the week go unused. Consider this option if you don't think you'd be able to use an exchange in the next two years.

Rental Summary

With all the difficulties associated with finding a renter yourself, collecting and paying taxes, and possibly incurring the liability of a damaged unit, it's usually not worth renting your week yourself. Exceptions include renting to friends or family or renting points.

If you decide to rent your week, only rent it yourself if you own a popular week. Furthermore, don't expect to make a profit unless you own a very high demand week. A reasonable goal is to try and cover your maintenance fees. Advertise on websites specializing in timeshare rentals. Rent out your week only if you can't use it and wouldn't be able to use the week that you would receive in exchange for your week.

Even before you acquire a timeshare, consider your exit strategy. For a variety of reasons, at some point you may decide that you no longer want to own your week. Timeshare sales people often tout the ability to eventually resell your week as a key feature of ownership. However, in reality, selling a timeshare often presents insurmountable difficulties. That's the biggest problem  with timeshares – getting rid of them when you no longer need or want them. Disposing of a timeshare takes time and if you try and sell your week, you probably won't be paid near as much as you'd like. It's much more difficult to sell a timeshare than to buy one. Set realistic expectations because you may not even be able to give your week away.

> "Buying a timeshare is a lot like marriage - easy to get into, and difficult and expensive to get out of. We recommend a long engagement!"
>
> *--TUG Moderator "DeniseM"*

Why Get Rid of Your Timeshare?

It's hard to imagine when you're focused on buying your dream timeshare that you'd ever want to get rid of it. Realistically, situations change and owners eventually dispose of their timeshares for a variety of reasons. Some people experience changes in their family situation. Others become disappointed with the resort, or change their vacationing patterns. Many sellers don't want to continue paying increasing maintenance fees or special assessments. Some of us even have an addiction to timesharing that results in owning more timeshares than we can use. Hopefully, you'll find someone to pay you for your timeshare when you no longer want to own it. If not, consider other options described below.

Disposal Options

There are several methods for getting rid of a timeshare and terminating your obligation. Most people would prefer to sell their timeshare if they can. Some owners buy RTU memberships using their current deeded timeshare as part of the payment. However, when selling becomes difficult, some people give their timeshare away – either by donating to a charity, by giving their ownership to someone that wants it, or by deeding the week back to the resort. Owners that ignore their obligation may lose their ownership through a foreclosure process. Desperate owners sometimes resort to extreme measures such as paying companies that specializes in eliminating the owner's commitment or placing the ownership in legal limbo.

Selling

Salespeople often list the ability to resell a timeshare as a beneficial feature of purchasing. However, few owners successfully sell their week for more than a fraction of what they paid, especially if they bought retail from a developer. The most difficult aspect of selling is finding a buyer that understands timeshare resales and is willing to pay a price acceptable to you. Unfortunately, an efficient secondary market for timeshare purchasing and selling does not yet exist. Many unscrupulous companies prey on desperate owners anxious to sell their timeshares. However, there are legitimate resale companies and licensed brokers that may be able to help you sell your week. If you deal with a company that helps owners sell their timeshares, don't pay any up-front fees other than small advertising fees.

Converting to Points

One option for owners of deeded timeshares, depending on where they own, may be to convert their deeded week to a points system that provides more flexibility and may make it easier to eventually sell. Although the conversion does not rid the owners of their timeshare, it may make the experience more enjoyable for them because of the added flexibility. The point system managers charge for this privilege (often thousands of dollars). Some people decide not to convert because of concerns over the future value of the points or distrust in managers that might oversell points to the point where there's limited availability. Some points systems technically prohibit the resale of points, but do allow for transfers to another member's account. In many cases, it's easier to sell points than to sell a fee-simple deeded ownership.

Donating to a Charity

If you want to get rid of your timeshare and help others at the same time, consider donating your timeshare to a charity. The donation provides resources to a needy cause, rids you of an unwanted timeshare, and possibly provides you a small tax deduction. However, some well-meaning donors actually create a burden for their cause if the charitable organization has no familiarity with liquidating a timeshare donation. Charities must fi nd a way to monetize the donation. For example, a local PBS station may include a timeshare donation in a fundraising auction.

Some owners erroneously believe that the financial benefits of a donation justify that choice. Unfortunately, few scenarios exist where this is true. However, if you have a charitable motive, donating the week may be a good option that helps eliminates your burden and benefits the charity. If you really want to do something nice for the charity, sell the timeshare yourself and then donate the cash proceeds.

Giving Away to Someone Other Than a Charity

Another option for disposing of your timeshare is to give it to someone. Unless you already know a person who wants your timeshare, advertise on websites like TUG and TimeshareForums with listings of free timeshares to attract a potential accepter. If friends or relatives express an interest in your timeshare, make sure they understand the commitment that they're making. Consider renting the week to them for the cost of the maintenance fees so that they can familiarize themselves with the experience before committing.

Another form of giving away a timeshare is to list it on eBay for $1 with no reserve price. To minimize closing costs, consider performing the closing yourself by requesting the estoppels letter, preparing and recording the deed, and then processing the resort transfer. Some desperate owners offer to pay for a professional closing agency's fees to reassure the person taking the week that all the paperwork has been properly filed.

Deeding Back / Deed in Lieu

Some resorts take weeks back and resell them rather than risking having to foreclose on an owner who has unpaid maintenance fees. They may also accept the deed to avoid a situation where there are unpaid maintenance fees in the future.

The resort may accept your deed as payment for an existing debt such as unpaid maintenance fees or special assessments. It's sometimes called a deedback or deed in lieu because you give them the deed (your ownership) in place of something like owed maintenance fees.

When you deed your timeshare back to the resort, they may pay the closing costs for preparing and recording the deed that transfers ownership back to them. However, they may insist that you pay those expenses or they may not even accept a deedback. A disappointing irony lies in the fact that some of the same resorts that promote the great value of their weeks refuse to take them back for free.

The deedback approach is a friendlier alternative to a legal foreclosure process. It saves the resort legal fees and enables them to attempt to resell the week sooner. Deeding the timeshare back to the resort may also provide them with an opportunity to redefine how weeks are controlled before they resell them, possibly with new deed restrictions or a different ownership model such as RTU. The resort is already familiar with your week and may already have a closing company that they work with. Therefore, they are in the best position to resell or rent out unused or returned weeks. However, if the resort winds up owning weeks that they can't sell or rent, the result is higher costs for the remaining owners.

Foreclosure

If you stop paying your maintenance fees, the resort will eventually foreclose on your week. This process costs the resort legal fees and may negatively impact your credit. However, if you don't have the money to pay the maintenance fees, the resort refuses to take the week back, and you are not worried about your credit rating, you might want to stop paying maintenance fees and wait for them conduct the foreclosure. It's possible that you could still owe unpaid fees as a debt even after the foreclosure. Before you pursue the foreclosure option, you may want to communicate your plan to the resort. They may be willing to consider a deedback to avoid the lengthy and expensive foreclosure process.

Paying to Take

Some companies specialize in helping desperate timeshare owners get rid of their timeshares. They often host seminars in local hotels where they explain how they can eliminate the current owner's commitment. They usually charge a fee of thousands of dollars. Although these companies appear to offer an easy way out (for a fee), you must be careful to ensure that they fulfill their obligation. These companies usually claim that they'll resell your week to get the ownership out of your name. One problem with this approach is that these companies typically dump the owner's week by listing it for $1 on eBay, potentially hurting resale values for other owners trying to sell. Try and sell the week yourself before paying large sums to a company.

Placing the Week in Legal Limbo

One extreme option is to transfer ownership of an unwanted week into a shell corporate entity such as a limited liability company (LLC) to sever the direct personal ownership relationship. By eliminating the direct tie to the current owner, a foreclosure of the unit may not hurt the owner's credit rating or result in continued debt.

Many consider this approach irresponsible as it negatively impacts fellow owners (represented by the HOA) because they must pay your share of expenses until the week is eventually foreclosed on. Costs for the owner may include setting up the entity, quitclaiming the ownership to the entity, and paying any resort transfer fees. The primary advantage of using this approach is that the timeshare is no longer tied directly to you personally. However, this option is time-consuming, costly, and is considered unethical by some. It may not be legal to convey ownership of an asset to a legal entity to avoid a debt. Consult with an attorney before pursuing this approach.

Selecting a Disposal Option

The strategy you select for disposing of your timeshare should depend on its value. Unless you have a valuable week, don't expect to sell it. If you own a timeshare that's not highly valued, you will find that there's not much of a secondary market for resales. It's difficult, if not impossible, to sell a low value timeshare such as an older resort, one in a poor location, or an off-season week. However, it never hurts to try and sell it before moving on to other options.

Disposal options include: selling, including paying someone (a professional resale broker) to sell it for you, or giving it away. Table 12 shows how the quality of the timeshare and your patience level may influence the option you select. Table 13 summarizes popular options in order of most to least desirable.

Table 12. Disposal Option Recommendations

Ownership Type	First Try	Settle For
Low-end Deeded	Donate	Deed back
Mid-level Deeded	Sell on your own	Donate
High-level Deeded	Sell on your own	Assisted sale
Points	Sell on your own	Assisted sale

Table 13. Timeshare Disposal Option Summary

Disposal Option	Advantages	Disadvantages
Sell	Partially reimburses purchase costs	Difficult to find buyers
Convert to points	Changes arrangement to provide more flexibility	Conversion process often costly
Donate to a charity	Potentially generates a tax deduction	Difficult to find charity that will accept
Give it away	Benefits recipient	Difficult to find someone to take it
Deed in lieu	Removes commitment obligations	Requires resort to accept deed
Foreclosure	No actions required on owners part	Hurts credit rating and burdens other owners
Pay to take	Eliminates commitment	High cost and risk that transaction may not be completed
Legal limbo	Eliminates commitment	Burdens fellow owners

Selling Process

The selling process for timeshares is similar to traditional real estate. Successful selling requires understanding what you're offering for sale, setting a price, finding a buyer, documenting the agreement, completing the sale, and paying the taxes on any profits. Figure 17 summarizes the selling process.

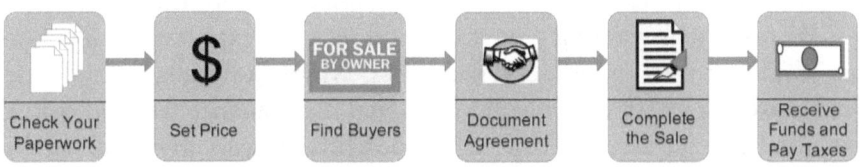

Figure 17. Selling Process

Understand What You're Selling

Before you begin the sales process, make sure you understand what you're selling and the rules that affect your sale. Refresh your memory on the details about your ownership so that you can accurately communicate them to potential  buyers. For example, recheck the status of your maintenance fees and when your unit can be used next. Fully disclose everything that you know to prospective buyers. Check your documents to see if the resort has a Right of First Refusal (ROFR) option. If you're unsure, ask your resort clarifying questions.

Setting a Price

If you advertise your week for sale, set a reasonable asking price. If you auction your week, determine a minimum bid or reserve price. Perform some research before you set your price,  keeping in mind that your week may be practically worthless. Set your price lower than your competitors.

Don't use the price you paid a developer as the basis for your resale price. You don't need to recover the same overhead costs as a developer. Understand the subtleties of the ownership you're selling such as views or restricted seasons and their impact on value. Ask your resort how they describe your week and what similar ones are selling for on the resale market.

Obtain a realistic expectation of value by performing some homework. Look online for the asking price for similar weeks. Make sure you're comparing your week to similar weeks in terms of size and type. When you look at resale prices, remember that these are weeks that have not been sold yet and may be overpriced. Some websites may mark listings as sold but provide no indication of the actual purchase price – only the original asking price. Completed eBay auctions provide a good source for determining current values, as well as reasonable selling prices for your unit.

Be realistic in valuing your week and set your expectations low. You may find that your timeshare is worthless. Many lower quality and older resorts are not worth committing to annual maintenance fees and risking potential special assessments. Also, potential buyers may realize that they can rent units at your resort without a commitment for less than the maintenance fees that they would have to pay as owners.

Set your price lower than all other posted listings for the same type of week. You can sweeten the deal for a potential buyer by conveying any associated banked exchange weeks as part of the transaction. Consider offering to pay closing costs or performing the closing yourself to entice a buyer. State in your ad that your price and terms are negotiable.

Finding a Buyer

Finding a buyer is the hardest part of the selling process and may bring you into contact with scam artists. Popular options for finding buyers include advertising, word of mouth, and using a broker. Because it's often hard to find a buyer, sellers sometimes employ the help of others.

Avoid Selling-Related Scams and Misleading Offers

Most timeshare-related scams and misleading offers target owners trying to dispose of their weeks. Many desperate timeshare sellers easily fall victim to scam artists. When you advertise your week for sale, you typically provide contact information such as your e-mail address or phone number in the advertisement. Unfortunately, this allows unscrupulous individuals and less-than-honorable companies to contact you, armed with the knowledge that you're trying to get rid of a timeshare. Your contact information may even be aggregated into mailing lists and sold to companies that contact timeshare sellers.

> "If it sounds too good to be true, it usually is"
>
> -- Catchphrase attributed to
> Better Business Bureau

Scam artists often look for owners who are desperate to rent or sell their timeshare. You may be contacted by someone that offers to help you dispose of your week. Timeshare owners are often approached through e-mail, phone calls, and by mail.

Popular timeshare scams and questionable practices include unsolicited offers to:

- Help you find buyers,
- Take over responsibility for your timeshare,
- Purchase your timeshare at a meeting, and
- Pay more than the asking price in return for a refund of the overpayment.

Assisting in Finding Buyers

Someone may contact you and try and sell you an advertising package for an up-front fee with no promises other than to continue advertising the week until it sells. The correspondence may give you the false impression that you'll be able to sell your timeshare for a high price. They may claim that they recently sold a timeshare similar to yours and only need a small fee to list yours the same way as the one that successfully sold. They might say that they will guarantee to find a buyer or refund your fee. They may even claim that they know someone that wants to buy your timeshare and that you only need to pay them a finder's fee and the closing costs to sell your week and obtain the sales proceeds.

However, once you give them your money, they don't have any reason to continue to work for you. They may only add your timeshare to their online listings on their website. Companies that you pay up-front fees, sometimes disguised as commissions, appraisal fees, or an advertising fee, have little incentive to help you sell your timeshare. In reality, the company probably does not have a buyer for your timeshare.

Taking Over Responsibility

Some companies offer to take over responsibility for your week for a fee of several thousand dollars, without following through on the promise to terminate your ownership. A company may invite you to a seminar where they disparage the timeshare concept and provide misleading information about the disadvantages of owning a timeshare. They may falsely state at the meeting that your loss on the sale of your unit is tax deductible. They may tell you that if you pay them to take the week, that they will take over responsibility for the commitment and then sell it themselves.

In reality, the company you meet with may require you to pay them to accept your limited power of attorney to try and sell your timeshare for you. You may find that the company turns over the timeshare to another company to sell. In cases where they promise to take over responsibility for your timeshare, they may never record a new deed nor make the transfer with the resort. If the company fails to find a new buyer for your timeshare before maintenance fees are due, expect to pay the fees and taxes yourself.

Baiting into an Up-Sell Presentation

Some companies search for vulnerable consumers to buy products they're selling such as travel discount clubs. They contact owners trying to sell their timeshares and offer to buy the week at a meeting in a local hotel. The company may say they want to purchase at the meeting and that the owners should bring their deed.

When the sellers arrive at the meeting to discuss the transaction with the company, the company attempts to sell something. The company may tie the purchase of the week to buying their overpriced product or service. The company probably doesn't really want the timeshare. The price they offer for their product or service may be the same as if the sellers weren't trading in their week.

"Send Me the Difference" Scam

Some scammers offer to send you more than your asking price and ask you to send them the difference. A scammer may contact you and sound very interested in buying your timeshare. As part of the negotiations, they may make up a story about needing to transfer funds and may offer to buy your timeshare for more that you're asking. The catch is that they want you to send them the difference between what they're paying and your asking price. In reality, the scam artists pay with a worthless check and they cash your refund check before your bank discovers that their inflated purchase price check is no good.

Avoiding Scams

When you advertise your week for sale or rent on a website, you typically list your e-mail address or other contact information. This enables scam artists to approach you in order to take advantage of you. Consider setting up a temporary e-mail account just for listing in your advertisement. Be suspicious if you receive unsolicited phone calls or e-mails. Be careful and make sure you know who you're dealing with. Don't be pressured into any immediate decisions. Before agreeing to meet someone, ascertain whether they're selling something.

Most experts warn against paying up-front fees for help with selling or renting your timeshare. Only pay small up-front fees (less than $100) to list your ad with well-known legitimate advertising companies. Under some situations, it's illegal for a company to collect an advance fee for listing a timeshare for sale.

If you own a valuable week and want help selling it, use a licensed broker or legitimate resale company that works on commission and only gets paid out of the proceeds of the actual sale. If you decide to pay someone to take over your week, think twice before signing a power of attorney. Sign a sales contract that requires them to record the accepted deed. Be suspicious if a company doesn't accept credit cards or distribute business cards with accurate current information. One strategy for dealing with companies requesting up-front fees is to offer them a large commission out of the sale proceeds instead of paying them before the sale. Demand a sales contract, review it carefully, and contact your attorney for their expert advice. Consider obtaining additional opinions from the NTOA and timeshare forums such as TUG.

Don't accept more than you're asking for a rental or sale. Wait for the buyer's check to completely clear before you convey title, even if you're provided a cashier's check. If you use a closing company, you greatly reduce the risk of being cheated during the payment phase of the transaction.

Scam Remedies

If you are victimized by scammers, potential remedies include contacting the state attorney general and disputing credit card charges. Historically, many timeshare scams have occurred in Mexico. The Mexican Federal Attorney's Consumer Office, referred to as Profeco, helps prospective owners avoid scams and assists owners who are victims of Mexican timeshare scams. The Licensed Timeshare Resale Brokers Association (LTRB) website identifies helpful resources for dealing with timeshare scams.

Legitimate Selling Assistance from Brokers and Resale Companies

Some companies charge high fees to help you sell your timeshare, and only add your listing to their database so that your week shows up along with many others on their website. Make sure you understand what a company will do to help you sell your timeshare before you give them any money. If you want assistance selling your week, consult legitimate professionals who'll help you dispose of your timeshare. Consider using the resort's broker, a real estate broker, or a legitimate resale company.

Find out if your resort assists with resales. Some resorts use brokered sales to help owners find buyers in return for a commission. Resorts use either their own personnel or work with an outside broker. They may include your week, along with foreclosed weeks, in the pool of weeks they offer for sale. Some states treat timeshare resale assistance like traditional real estate.

Look for an agent who maintains a real estate license in the state where the resort is located. Surprisingly, not all real estate companies use licensed brokers. Check the Web for reviews or complaints about the broker or real estate company. While a resale assistance company may only be able to advertise for you, a licensed real estate broker can also support negotiations and assist with the sales process. *TimeSharing Today* periodically publishes a directory of licensed brokers. There is also a directory of licensed brokers on the website of the Licensed Timeshare Resale Brokers Association.

Some resale companies may try to charge you an up-front fee. Make sure you know what you're getting for your money before paying any up-front fees. A small advertising fee might be reasonable, but any large amount is highly questionable.

Advertising

Advertise or auction your week on your own or hire professional help. Do-it-yourself advertising options include enlisting the help of the resort, listing it in classified ads, networking, and posting to an auction site. First, choose between listing your week for sale and using an auction. The choice depends on how desperate or impatient you are. Try selling first and then auction the week if you lose patience.

Your resort may help you sell your week or at least provide effective suggestions. Check with them to see if they assist with selling or advertising. They may offer a resale program or advertising opportunities such as a bulletin board, newsletter, or website. However, you may find yourself in competition with the resort selling foreclosed weeks, so they might not be interested in helping you sell your week unless you employ their broker.

List your week for sale using free and low-cost websites and publications. Advertise with timeshare media such as *TimeSharing Today* and on timeshare community websites such as TUG or Timeshare Forums. Craigslist has become the most popular classified ad system on the Web. Their listings are free and are geographically oriented because of the way the site is organized. Place Craigslist ads in the website sections for the resort's location, your area, and major population centers within driving distance of the resort. Also consider advertising with online websites specializing in selling timeshares such as RedWeek.com. Double check your advertisement to ensure that all details are accurate.

The best pool of qualified buyers is people already familiar with your resort. Fellow owners, former tenants, and friends and family who have joined you for vacations already understand the features and amenities of your particular timeshare. When you visit the resort, casually mention to your fellow guests at the bar or pool that you're trying to sell your week.

Online auctions are a popular option for desperate sellers. The largest auction website, eBay, provides an online *Timeshare Seller's Guide* to help sellers understand the process. Unlike most eBay bids, real estate auction bids on eBay are considered non-binding, which means technically you only agree to the buyer's interest in the terms with the auction and must follow up with the actual contractual agreement. Look at similar auction listings on eBay for ideas on pricing and presenting information.

Although you can set a minimum or reserve auction price, the odds of selling may increase if you start with a low price. Encourage your listing's popularity by setting a low minimum offer such as $1. List your timeshare in the real estate category of eBay. Pay the $35 (as of 2011) insertion fee for adding your timeshare auction listing. Instead of paying the typical 9% of the final bid at the end of an eBay auction, timeshares have a flat $35 notice fee if bids were received. If you set a higher initial price, you'll incur insertion fees, and you may not garner as much interest. When you construct your auction listing for eBay, look at content from similar timeshare listings, carefully avoiding errors in your listing by copying only applicable content. Consider eBay Superlister tools ($15 in 2011) to create a professional listing. Professional eBay sellers, called trading assistants, can help sell your timeshare for you on eBay. If you use an auction, expect a lower price but faster results than from listing it for sale.

There are legitimate companies that will help you advertise your timeshare for sale. However, some companies only advertise your week and forward responses to you. Referred to as Post Card Companies (PCC), some companies send unsolicited offers (often on postcards) offering to help you sell your timeshare. If you decide to hire professional assistance, look for someone who has successfully sold units at your resort. Find out how much they charge to help you and what specific services they will provide for their fee. Ensure that you understand whether you're hiring an advertising company or hiring a broker.

Communicating with Potential Buyers

If you're lucky enough to be contacted by a potential buyer, be responsive to their questions with accurate answers. Respond quickly to offers with a counter offer if necessary. You may need to educate the buyer if they're not familiar with timeshares. The easiest buyer to deal with is someone that already owns a week at your resort. Talk to the buyer about the purchase price and terms such as who will pay the closing costs. Keep your buyer engaged with frequent communications until you successfully complete the transaction.

Documenting the Agreement

Document your agreement regarding the terms of the sale in a written contract with the buyer. Follow the process outlined in the Buying section above. However, keep in mind that a seller's priorities differ from a buyer's. In the contract, specify

the price, payment terms, timeline, and any banked weeks conveyed with the transaction. A long contractual document can be intimidating to a buyer. Reassure them that you're using standard language, protecting both parties, and following legal requirements.

Document requirements vary depending on the location of the timeshare and the parties involved in the transaction. Resale document kits are available for purchase or from organizations such as the NTOA. The kits include templates for the paperwork you need to document the sales agreement. Certain states, like Florida, require specific language in some of the documents, so check that the contract is valid for the state where the timeshare is located.

Completing the Sale

Deed preparation and transfer processes vary widely. Buyers typically pay the closing costs arranged by the seller. However, which party pays for these fees can be negotiated. Closing companies, sometimes called closing agencies, provide services to help you complete the transaction. Unless you want to perform the transfer paperwork yourself, select a reputable but low cost closing agency.

If you're performing the closing process yourself, provide an estoppels letter as part of the process to reassure the buyer that you do indeed own what you claim to own and that all fees have been paid. If your condominium documents or contract provide the developer with the Right of First Refusal (ROFR) option, carefully follow the required process.

Closing companies typically escrow the funds and handle the paperwork for a few hundred dollars. By handling the collection and dispersion of funds, the closing company can help protect you from problems such as bad checks and unscrupulous buyers. Make sure you pay off any remaining loan or mortgage on the timeshare. If you still owe money on a financed timeshare purchase, the loan should be paid off as part of the transaction. If the proceeds of the sale aren't sufficient to pay off the loan, you must pay the difference to fulfill your financial obligations for the loan. You may be responsible for ownership commitments until the resort is informed and the transfer fee paid.

Payment and Taxes

The buyer or closing company will send you a check for the proceeds. Your tax liabilities from selling your week depend on several factors including whether you made or lost money and whether you used it exclusively for rental purposes. Determine the profit or loss for your timeshare sale by subtracting the cost basis from the sales price. If the resulting amount is negative, that means that you have a loss, and if the number is positive, you have a gain. For tax purposes, the cost basis includes closing costs and transfer fees. Other potential adjustments to the cost basis include reserves for capital improvements paid as part of maintenance fees, special assessments paid for capital improvements, and depreciation you claimed when you were renting out your week. Examples of profit and loss calculations without accounting for depreciation are shown in Table 14.

Table 14. Example Profit and Loss Calculations

Category	Components	Loss Example	Profit Example
Sales Price	Negotiated amount	$1,500	$1,000
Cost Basis	Price paid	$2,500	$500
	+ closing costs	$500	$300
	+ transfer fees	$100	$100
	Total cost basis	$3,100	$900
Profit / Loss	Profit (sales Price – total cost basis)		$100 profit ($1,000 - $900)
	Loss (total cost basis – sales price)	$1,600 loss ($3,100 - ($1,500)	

In the unlikely event that you actually make a profit on the sale of your timeshare, don't forget to pay the capital gains taxes. If you profit from a timeshare that you own for longer than a year, you may be able to treat the profit as a long term capital gain.

Unfortunately, you most likely can't deduct a loss because a timeshare is treated like a personal asset unless you used it for a long period of time as a rental business. A timeshare you or your family or friends use or exchange is considered a personal use timeshare. If you lose money from selling a personal use timeshare, you can't deduct the loss. In some situations, such as buying the timeshare only to try and flip it for a business profit, the loss might be deductible.

If you've been using your timeshare exclusively as a rental (business use) for some time, the tax consequences are different. Consider a timeshare you regularly rent out as a rental timeshare. If you lose money on the sale of a rental use timeshare, it may be considered a deductible business loss. Since only the losses on rental use timeshares are deductible, it may be tempting to convert your personal use timeshare into a rental use timeshare prior to selling it. However, you may have to use the lesser of the value when you purchased the timeshare or the value when you converted it from personal use to business to determine the amount of the loss. The IRS may look back to see if you declared rental income during the years you claim you were using your week as a rental. Think about renting for several consecutive years prior to the sale to demonstrate that the timeshare is a rental and not a personal use timeshare.

Most people receive less for their timeshare than they paid and don't realize a taxable profit. Sellers who do profit usually have been using their timeshare for personal use, and not exclusively as a rental business. People who pay a high price (usually to a developer) and rent out for several consecutive years may realize a small deduction for their taxes when they resell their week.

Figure 18 provides a flowchart of the potential tax consequences of selling your timeshare. There are many factors involved and you should consult a tax professional to discuss your particular situation.

Point Conversion Process

When you convert a deeded week to a point system, the points company evaluates your week and assigns its value as a number of annual points. Review your options for using that number of points at the current rates. Keep in mind that the managing company may change the number of points you need to access their resorts in the future. The conversion process is similar to buying into a points system, except that you're trading in your existing deed-based week as part of the payment.

Depending on the points system, you may pay a conversion fee and surrender your deed. Think twice before you pay a large fee to the resort to convert to a points system. It might be cheaper to sell your week and buy a

131

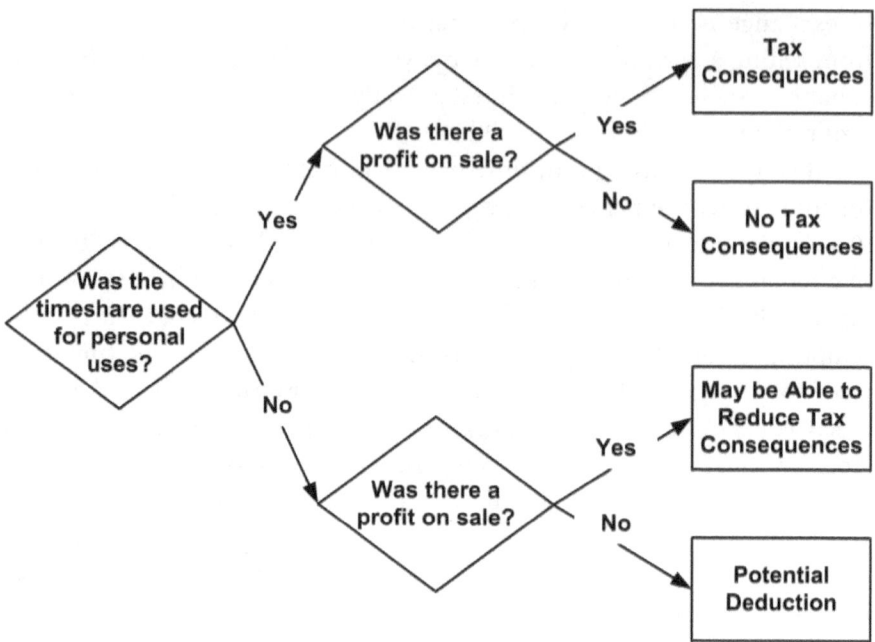

Figure 18. Tax Consequences at Sale

resale points membership. In some cases, you keep your deeded week and add points as an option. Adding a points option doesn't eliminate your timeshare ownership, but does give you more ways to access resorts.

Process for Donating a Timeshare

Donating your week to charity involves finding a charity that accepts donations, transferring ownership, accounting for the tax deduction. Some organizations advertise that they selectively accept timeshare donations.

Some timeshare brokers and donation-assistance companies will sell your timeshare, and then forward the proceeds to your designated charity. Before you donate your timeshare, pay off any mortgage or loan and ensure that the maintenance fees are paid.

Finding a Charity

Most charities gladly accept the money that results from selling your timeshare. However, few are interested in accepting a timeshare donation that they must sell. One of the toughest aspects of donating is finding a charity that will directly accept the donation. Some charities advertise their willingness to accept timeshare donations, although they may restrict which timeshares they accept. They may reject some donation offers because low value weeks are difficult for them to sell. Some charities may refer you to a timeshare resale company that they use. It's easier for a charity to monetize a points donation and the process is simpler for you. However, since it's easier to sell points than weeks, consider selling the points yourself and giving the money to the charity.

Making the Donation

Some charities document their timeshare donation policies and procedures on their website. They should provide you a receipt or letter for your tax records indicating their tax exempt status. Assuming the charity accepts timeshare donations directly, make sure you know how they'll handle changing the ownership and how long you must continue to pay the annual maintenance fees. Some charities request a fee to offset their cost for selling your week.

Some charities work with companies that specialize in handling timeshare donations. These companies sell the week, process the paperwork, and give the proceeds to the charity on your behalf. They also arrange for the charity to send you a receipt letter to document your donation. Donation assistance companies appear to provide a generous service. However, they may have close ties to a required closing company that profits from handling the eventual sale. Also, they may receive a portion of the sale price for their service. Follow up to ensure that the deed was correctly recorded and that the transfer was documented in the resort's records. You may want to time your donation to coincide with tax season deadlines.

Tax Implications

IRS regulations allow you to deduct the fair market value of a donated timeshare. Remember that this tax benefit is much smaller, depending on your tax bracket, than the amount you could obtain from selling the timeshare. Seek advice from your tax accountant or attorney about the tax implications of donating your timeshare. The donation may or may not be considered deductible. Treat deeded weeks as real estate donations and treat donated points memberships as personal property donations. If you successfully donate a deeded timeshare week to a charity, determine the amount of the deduction by assessing the fair market value (FMV) of the week on the date the timeshare was donated. The FMV is the price that you would have received had you resold the timeshare to someone else. Since resale prices normally fall considerably below developer prices, your deduction may be much less than the price you paid to a developer.

Determining and Documenting FMV

Determining FMV often presents a significant challenge. Because timeshare appraisals can be relatively expensive and cannot be included as part of the donation deduction, most owners forgo them. A good determination of FMV, however, is the price that the charity receives from a buyer. If the week sells before you file your tax return, use the sales price as the FMV. Unfortunately, it may sell for very little or not sell at all before you need a dollar figure. Remember that the FMV of a timeshare week is based on its resale price, not what a developer charges. If you donate a timeshare that's worth more than you paid for it, the FMV is the price you paid, not the potential resale price. If you donate a Right to Use timeshare or a membership in a non-deeded points based timeshare, the IRS rules regarding tangible personal property must be followed.

If you want to claim that the timeshare's worth exceeds $5,000, you're required to have an appraisal. However, unlike year-round real estate, it usually doesn't make sense to do an appraisal on a timeshare, donation. You cannot add the appraisal costs to the value of the deduction. Donations worth less than $5,000 don't require an appraisal but should still be substantiated through documented research.

Tax Bracket Implications

A timeshare deduction may lower your adjusted gross income (the basis for determining your taxes) not the amount you pay in taxes. The benefit of the deduction is based on your tax bracket and assumes that you itemize your deductions. For example, if the FMV is $1,000 and your effective tax rate is 20%, you only receive a $200 advantage by claiming the deduction. Even if you were to sell the timeshare for half of its fair market value ($500 in this example), you'd be better off selling it than obtaining the tax deduction ($200 in this example). The lower your effective tax rate, the less the deduction helps you financially. Table 15 provides examples of the impact of tax rates on deductions.

Table 15. Sample Scenarios for Donating Instead of Selling

	Example #1	Example #2
Fair Market Value	$1,000	$1,000
Seller's effective tax rate	15%	20%
Financial value of deduction	$150	$200
Potential quick sale price	$500	$500
Benefit of selling instead of donating	$350	$300

You might want to donate your timeshare for convenience or for charitable motives. Handing off a timeshare to a charity provides many people a stress-free method for eliminating their commitment. However, remember that the value of a tax deduction is dependent on your tax bracket and the taxable income that's effectively reduced by the fair market value of the deduction. Therefore, from a purely economic perspective, you're better off selling instead of donating. If your primary incentive is the warm feeling you receive from knowing you did something to help the charity's causes, sell the week yourself and donate the cash proceeds.

Process for Giving Away Timeshares

If you experience difficulty finding a buyer, give the week away to someone other than a charity. Like other recyclables, make sure you responsibly dispose of an unwanted timeshare. Don't force others to pay for your poor decisions. The process for giving away your week depends on whether you bequeath it, deed it back, give it to a new owner, pay someone to take it, encourage foreclosure, or place it in legal limbo.

Bequeath it to Someone in Your Will

You may own your timeshare until the day you die. Timeshares often change hands as a result of the owners passing away. Many owners bequeath their timeshares as part of their estate. If your timeshare is deeded, your estate may be probated in both the state of residency and the state where the resort is located. If the recipients don't want the timeshare and they're not listed on the deed, they don't have to accept the timeshare as part of their inheritance after your death. An RTU membership is treated like personal property in an estate.

Process for Deeding back to the Resort

Contact the resort and ask if they take weeks back. The resort may agree to take the week but require that you pay the associated closing costs of changing ownership. You probably don't need a contract in this situation. Resorts or their closing agent will send you paperwork to sign and return. The paperwork may include a quitclaim deed or warranty deed that requires witnesses and notarized signatures. Make photocopies of everything. Once you return the paperwork, the closing agent will record the deed transfer with the local government office and the resort will reflect the change in their records.

Process for Giving to a New Owner

You might find someone that's willing to take over your ownership obligation which includes future maintenance fees. TUG has an area on their website where owners can advertise free weeks. Also, look for individuals who advertise that they are willing to take certain weeks. If you give your timeshare to a friend or relative, make sure they understand the commitment they're taking on. It could hurt your relationship if they blame you for encouraging them to get into a commitment that they later regret.

Consider offering to take it back from them if they ever regret the decision, or rent it to them for the cost of the maintenance fees until they're comfortable becoming owners. The closing process should be similar to selling the week.

Process for Paying Someone to Take Your Timeshare

If all other methods fail, consider using an organization that you pay to dispose of your timeshare for you. For example, one company demands seven times the annual maintenance fees as payment for them to take your timeshare. Although this approach incurs a considerable cost, it might quickly and conveniently rid you of your commitment. The expensive service may be worth it to some people to eliminate a headache.

Some owners that have paid for this type of service have been disappointed to learn that they still own the timeshare they thought they disposed of. Make sure the company is contractually bound to perform the transfer and not just try to help sell your timeshare. If they insist on being paid by check instead of using a credit card option, it may be a warning sign that they can't be trusted. Another warning sign is if they don't have business cards or have inaccurate or non-existent contact information on the card. After the agreed upon and documented period of time, contact the resort to make sure that the company transferred the ownership out of your name. Before you pay a company to take your timeshare, offer the same payment to your resort. If they aren't willing to accept a simple deed back or deed in lieu, they might accept this type of offer.

Process for Allowing or Encouraging Foreclosure

Deed foreclosure can be an expensive legal process for a resort. Foreclosing on a non-deeded interest is much simpler because it doesn't involve complex real estate legal issues. Owners who stop paying maintenance fees lose their access rights and the resort is eventually forced to foreclose on the timeshare to regain ownership. The owner loses their timeshare as a result of the foreclosure process and may suffer negative impacts to their credit history.

You may think that abandoning your timeshare responsibilities is equivalent to giving it back to the developer or HOA because they'll eventually regain control of the week through their foreclosure process. However, it's better to offer to voluntarily deed the timeshare back to the resort so that they can resell the week. If the resort won't accept the deed back and you stop paying maintenance fees, they may be forced to perform a foreclosure. Remember that you made a commitment and dispose of your week in a responsible way.

Process for Placing Your Timeshare Into Legal Limbo

By deeding an unwanted timeshare to an LLC or similar entity, the owner effectively walks away and limits their personal liability. The process involves forming a shell company with no assets and then giving the timeshare to that company. In some states, you can easily create an LLC online. Once the entity is established, you can quit-claim the deed to the LLC. The new deed must be accepted by the owners or managers of the entity for the transaction to be completed. When considering this approach, consider telling the resort your intentions and offering them a final chance to take the week back. Think hard about whether this option is an ethical alternative as it saddles other owners with an increased share of costs until the week can be eventually foreclosed on by the resort. Also, contact your attorney to make sure that this approach would be legal for you.

Alternatives to Disposing of Timeshares

If you're unable to get rid of your timeshare, you have some options. You can continue using the timeshare with your friends and family. You might be able to convert it to a points-based system. You can exchange it each year to access another timeshare. You could also rent out the timeshare. Continuing to own only to exchange effectively raises your annual cost. This is because you're paying maintenance fees, exchange company membership dues, and exchange fees every year. It might make more sense in this situation to sell it and buy a points-based timeshare.

Disposal Summary

If you want to dispose of your timeshare, have realistic expectations. It takes time to dispose of your week and you probably won't receive as much money as you paid initially, especially if you bought from a developer. Be wary of potential scams and don't pay up-front fees. Consider trying to sell your week, then explore other options if it doesn't sell.

Chapter 7
The Future of Timesharing

What does the future hold for timeshares? Eventually, you may be able to buy underwater or space timeshares. However, in the near term, timeshare business models will continue to evolve and new solutions will be found for aging timeshares.

Why Worry About the Future?

People buy timeshares based on assumptions about the future – especially the anticipated cost of accessing similar accommodations. They have expectations about how they plan on using, exchanging, renting out, and eventually disposing of their timeshare.

Recognizing Realities about Timesharing

Understanding the future of timeshares requires recognizing and accepting the realities that impact trends. These realities include slowing construction of new units and depreciating existing resorts. Aging owners are paying maintenance fees that they may find burdensome as they struggle to rent or dispose of their weeks in an inefficient market.

Developers Have Fewer New Units to Sell

In some places, such as areas of southwest Florida, it is increasingly difficult to obtain zoning approval for new timeshare properties. This scarcity may eventually lead to shortages in supply as developers run out of places to locate new developments, especially on the beach. Until recently, the increasing value of land and use rights (zoning) reduced the availability of potential sites for building timeshare resorts in specific areas.

The economic downturn that began in 2008 led to a reduction in demand which caused many timeshare companies to downsize and slow or stop construction of new units. It may be years before we see a major resurgence in timeshare resort development. Developers may wind up selling largely from an inventory of foreclosed weeks or weeks they acquire by exercising ROFR options. The recession also affected resale prices – creating incredible buying opportunities for those who can afford the ongoing costs.

Depreciating Resorts Require Renovation

As development of new timeshares slows, the average age of existing timeshares increases. Aging, depreciating resorts require maintenance fees to keep them from deteriorating. The impact of the initial purchase price quickly gives way to awareness of the ongoing expense of annual maintenance fees. If maintenance fee costs rise above the rental cost, potential buyers have less incentive to buy instead of rent. Alternatively, if resorts don't collect adequate revenues through maintenance fees, they cannot properly maintain the resort.

Aging timeshares require major renovations. Many developers built timeshare resorts with short term objectives. Others converted older motels or apartment complexes into timeshare resorts. As these properties age, they require extensive updates to maintain their appeal. At some point, they need to be either majorly renovated or retired. With declining desirability, resorts struggle to retain maintenance fee-paying owners.

Aging Owners Struggle with their Financial Committment

The burden for maintaining and renovating aging timeshares is borne by owners around the world that own millions of timeshare weeks. These owners' situations change as they age and eventually pass away. Many people see their disposable income go down as they retire. However, maintenance fees typically increase each year. Also, owners on fixed incomes may be surprised with special assessments. The financial commitment of their timeshare ownership can easily become burdensome. Additionally, the reasons owners had for buying may no longer affect their ownership decisions as they get older.

Timeshare Rental and Resale Markets are Inefficient

Unfortunately, when owners recognize that they can no longer afford their ownerships, it is often difficult for them to rent or resell their weeks. Even well-maintained timeshares may be difficult to rent or sell. Once owners decide to dispose of their week, they often discover the difficulty of selling something with often minimal residual value. The fragmented resale market is also inefficient in matching buyers and sellers. The difficulty in disposing of timeshares has led to extreme options such as paying a company to take over the owner's responsibility.

The rental market is also inefficient. It's difficult to rent a timeshare week without resort participation. Although people successfully advertise and find renters, the extensive amount of work often results in only enough money to pay for the year's maintenance fees. If consumers were better educated and understood the value proposition of timeshare ownership and rentals, demand (and consequently prices) might increase.

"Nothing endures but change"

-- Heraclitus from
Lives of the Philosophers by Diogenes Laertius

Trends Affecting Timeshares

The timeshare concept is constantly changing and evolving. As buyers and owners become more educated and demanding, developers must modify their approaches. Changes result from lessons learned, increased access to information, improved automation, and social pressures. Developers modify their approaches and offerings respond to buyers' educations and desires.

Buyers and Owners are Increasingly Educated and Demanding

Timeshare buyers' expectations continue to rise. The desire for high quality resort accommodations is likely to continue increasing. New buyers often want high-end finishes and luxury amenities. Existing timeshares have the option of renovating or even rebuilding to lower their effective age and attract and retain owners, but this usually requires large special assessments. Demand for timeshares decreased following the 2008 recession, resulting in slowdowns among developers. The pace of supply increase has slowed. However, once the economy rebounds to the point that demand improves, there may eventually be limited value appreciation for owners that bought resale.

The increased amount of information available on the Web regarding resales, quality perceptions, and timeshare advantages and disadvantages is leading to more educated owners. There are many more educational resources available to timeshare owners than in the past. Owners and purchasers no longer rely solely on the claims of motivated salespeople at sales presentations. The Web provides access to more information and easily connects buyers with sellers and landlords with tenants.

The large numbers of timeshares listed for sale on the Web provide helpful references to owners attempting to determine the worth of their ownership. Although these listings communicate asking prices, they provide some reference points for owners. Some buyers and sellers share their purchase price and ROFR results with others in online forums.

Knowledge leads to action. Access to information results in more educated timeshare owners who become motivated to influence their resort's management. Owners often organize to pressure management companies to control costs, terminate older timeshares, or majorly renovate resorts at superior locations. Some owners groups even bring litigation against the developer or management company. Owners have different expectations than hotel guests. The younger generation especially demands more transparency, higher quality amenities, and more flexible options. Those trends favor points-based systems in the future.

As owners and managers consider their resorts' impact on the environment, they are adopting more socially conscious approaches. Like the hotel industry, timeshare resorts are increased emphasis on energy conservation and recycling. This trend reflects the growing importance to many owners of going green. Timeshares provide efficient use because of their high occupancy rates compared to wholly-owned condos and hotels. Energy conservation initiatives at resorts also help reduce the utility cost portion of maintenance fees for the owners.

Developers and Exchange Companies are Evolving

Developers are encouraged by their profit motives to respond to the demands and desires of increasingly informed potential buyers. Developers are offering new buyers more flexibility. As timeshare owners and potential purchasers learn about points-based access, demand for timeshares may increase. Large hospitality-oriented companies now sell most new timeshares in the form of points-based vacation clubs. This shift satisfies demands for flexibility instead of locking owners into fixed weeks or a single resort.

Exchange companies are also responding to their customers. Many exchangers claim that it is increasingly difficult to perform satisfactory exchanges. Many long time exchangers see a disappointing trend in dealing with exchange companies. They express frustration with the exchange process and the difficulty in finding what they consider to be equitable trades. Some believe that exchange companies' rental businesses compete for availability of quality units for exchanges. Others feel that the exchange companies have a conflict of interest when they attempt to rent deposited weeks rather than trying to find matches with customers looking for a trade.

Automation and information technology advances are helping resorts and exchange companies become more efficient and offer new features. Exchange companies like RCI are responding to dissatisfied exchangers by providing more information to members. Exchange values are becoming more transparent through point systems that clearly identify the relative value of a week an unit type. This approach explicitly values weeks being traded by offering a certain number of points for a week being deposited. The offered number of points takes into account the length of time until the check-in date as well as the desirability of the offered week. The best exchange system for owners would also present the point cost of accessing available weeks before the owner is required to deposit a week.

Predictions

The timeshare industry will evolve in new ways in response to consumer demands. Developers will make changes based on their lessons learned in dealing with potential buyers. Lawmakers may continue to change regulations to protect consumers and simplify foreclosure processes. As owners become more educated about their ownership, expect them to advocate for changes at their resorts. Also, expect them to change how they buy, use, exchange, rent out, and dispose of their timeshares in the future.

Increasingly Educated and Proactive Owners

Future timeshare purchasers will be armed with even more information about timeshares and how to effectively use them. Reliable sources of information will be accessed by consumers on the Web, as well as through traditional print media.

Owners need motivation to continue their responsibility. Resorts may need to discount the maintenance fees for low value weeks to ensure that owners of those weeks continue to pay. HOA boards depend on volunteer labor, although difficulties arise in recruiting volunteers to meet and represent owners in making decisions. A well-run management company minimizes requirements on HOA board members. Eventually, HOA board members may be paid or receive discounted maintenance fees in return for their participation. Social media tools such as Facebook enable owners to easily communicate with each other and build consensus on resort issues.

Owners may lobby state legislatures to update timeshare laws. In the past, timeshare legislation has focused on development and sales. As timeshares age, new laws are needed to help timeshare owners. For example, some timeshare require a 100% affirmative vote to terminate the timeshare, a highly unreasonable goal with so many owners and some of the ownerships tied up in bankruptcy, foreclosure, and probate. New laws will continue to simplify the foreclosure process. For example, Florida recently passed a law that authorizes streamlined process for uncontested non-judicial foreclosures.

Improved Business Models and Marketplaces

Developers will continue to make changes to entice educated buyers. Points, ever more popular, provide flexibility to consumers with busy unpredictable schedules. RTU approaches provide a useful alternative to owning a deeded timeshare in perpetuity. New timeshares may eventually consist primarily of non-deeded, right-to-use ownerships with points access models to provide transparency and flexibility.

Existing deeded timeshare resorts may evolve towards this model. Resorts and their HOAs gain control over existing deeded timeshare weeks as they are returned through foreclosure or deed in lieu transactions. These resort owned deeded weeks could then be re-deeded as restricted right-to-use weeks. The resort could then sell those weeks to new owners as part of a non-deeded equity membership. This would provide the new owners the benefit of a limited ownership commitment, yet allow them to retain some control with ownership rights.

Developers will likely find new ways to market and sell timeshare ownership. For example, they may begin to use online videos to supplement tours and social media to obtain referrals. Existing owners will witness the improvements to the timeshare model and will look for ways to implement changes at existing resorts.

Improved Operations and Owner Support

Resorts are dependent on the owners to continue operating. Even resorts that are not controlled by HOAs recognize that they must be responsive to owners to keep them involved and paying maintenance fees. As a result of activist owners, resorts may evolve to operate more efficiently and to provide better ways to help owners rent and dispose of existing weeks.

Many timeshares, especially older properties, are managed like small stand-alone businesses. This leads to costly inefficiencies that negatively impact maintenance fees. Resorts could combine or outsource some functions, such as accounting, payroll, reservations, and other back-office services. Automation will provide efficient management of room nights including advertising, reservations, charges, and profit allocations to owners for rentals. Resorts will likely continue to provide more services to owners on the Web. Allowing owners to access information and make changes themselves without requiring support from employees at the resort saves money. Timeshare management companies and exchange companies will continue to provide more Web-based tools and mobile applications that allow owners to quickly and easily access information. Companies will continue to encourage owners to perform their own online transactions rather than calling a customer service agent on the phone.

Eventually, owners may gain equity participation as shareholders in corporations that own resorts or become members in cooperatives that resemble existing organization models such as credit unions. These arms length relationships could limit owner liability and lead to a different sense of responsibility, commitment, and volunteerism. Regardless of the ownership type, changes are needed so that people can terminate their commitment easier. Furthermore, new laws are needed to simplify the process of ending old timeshares.

As timeshare owners look for more flexibility with their ownership, they may pressure management companies to work harder at renting their units. Timeshare management companies may act more proactively to help owners rent their weeks. Renters want to trust who they are sending money to – not merely an owner with a Craigslist advertisement. Resorts and their management companies are best equipped to help rent weeks. Ideally, timeshares would be operated more like condo-hotels with 52 owners per unit. However, this is a paperwork nightmare. Anticipate new software technology to alleviate this problem. Many older properties need to move into the Internet age and use Web resources to educate and sell to potential renters. Partnerships with popular travel websites like Orbitz and Expedia will increase exposure to available timeshare units alongside hotel rooms. This will provide much-needed additional advertising to help renters find available owners' units.

Uninformed travelers may be disappointed by some of the differences between a hotel and a timeshare resort. From the first encounter, such as the website or a phone call, the resort or travel services company should set the expectation level of the guest. At check-in, the timeshare's operations and services should be briefly presented to non-owners. Perhaps by offering services such as daily maid service to renters, resorts may successfully compete directly for customers who desire luxurious accommodations and expect hotel style services.

Making Memories

The future of timeshares is uncertain, but one thing is definite. You can make incredible memories with your friends and family at your timeshare. Many educated owners continue to enjoy their resorts and are proud of their decision to purchase their timeshare. You can determine your own timesharing future by deciding whether to buy, use, and enjoy a timeshare. Remember to consider buying resale and keep in mind that you're making a long term commitment. If you carefully make educated decisions, timeshares represent a cost-effective way to enjoy luxury resort accommodations for many years to come.

Recommended Information Sources

Many timeshare information sources are biased, so try and determine the motives of the authors. Some Web content providers change their site's address making it difficult to access information. Therefore, rather than providing Web addresses that may change after printing, please reference this book's companion website for current Web address links.

Recommended Books and Magazines

- *Vacation Nation* by Elaine Joli
  ISBN 978-1439261378 (2009)
- *Timeshare Owners: Don't Get Scammed!*
  ISBN 978-1439244951 (2009)
- *The Everything Family Guide to Timeshares* by Kim Kavin
  ISBN 978-1593377113 (2006)
- *Timeshare Vacations for Dummies* by Lisa Ann Schreier
  ISBN 978-0764584428 (2005)
- *Surviving a Timeshare Presentation* by Lisa Ann Schreier
  ISBN 978-1932863123 (2004)
- *Timeshare Condominiums for the Beginner* by Michael Strauss
  ISBN 978-0533110384 (1995)
- *TimeSharing Today* magazine
- *Owners Perspective* magazine

Industry Information

- American Resort Development Association (ARDA)
- The Resort Trades magazine (for timeshare industry professionals)
- Licensed Timeshare Resale Brokers Association (LTRBA)

Timeshare Communities

- National Timeshare Owners' Association (NTOA)
- TimeshareForums
- Timeshare User's Group (TUG)

Links to these and other recommended resources are provided on the companion website:

http://www.usedtimesharesbook.com

U.S. Federal Holidays[1]

	2011	2012	2013	2014
New Year's Day	Friday 12/31/10	Monday 1/2/12	Tuesday 1/1/13	Wednesday 1/1/14
Birthday of Martin Luther King, Jr.	Monday 1/17/11	Monday 1/16/12	Friday 1/21/13	Monday 1/20/14
Washington's Birthday	Monday 2/21/11	Monday 2/20/12	Monday 2/18/13	Monday 2/17/14
Memorial Day	Monday 5/30/11	Monday 5/28/12	Monday 5/27/13	Monday 5/26/14
Independence Day	Monday 7/4/11	Wednesday 7/4/12	Thursday 7/4/13	Friday 7/4/14
Labor Day	Monday 9/5/11	Monday 9/3/12	Monday 9/2/13	Monday 9/1/14
Columbus Day	Monday 10/10/11	Monday 10/8/12	Monday 10/14/13	Monday 10/13/14
Veterans Day	Friday 11/11/11	Monday 11/12/12	Monday 11/11/13	Tuesday 11/11/14
Thanksgiving Day	Thursday 11/24/11	Thursday 11/22/12	Thursday 11/28/13	Thursday 11/27/14
Christmas Day	Monday 12/26/11	Tuesday 12/25/12	Wednesday 12/25/13	Thursday 12/25/14

1   Source: U.S. Office of Personnel Management

Canadian Federal Public Holidays[2]
(provincial holidays vary)

	2011	**2012**	**2013**	**2014**
New Year's Day	Saturday 1/1/11	Sunday 1/1/12	Tuesday 1/1/13	Wednesday 1/1/14
Good Friday	Friday 4/22/11	Friday 4/6/12	Friday 3/29/13	Friday 4/18/14
Easter Monday	Monday 4/25/11	Monday 4/9/12	Monday 4/1/13	Monday 4/21/14
Victoria Day	Monday 5/23/11	Monday 5/21/12	Monday 5/20/13	Monday 5/19/14
Canada Day	Friday 7/1/11	Sunday 7/1/12	Monday 7/1/13	Tuesday 7/1/14
Labour Day	Monday 9/5/11	Monday 9/3/12	Monday 9/2/13	Monday 9/1/13
Thanksgiving Day	Monday 10/10/11	Monday 10/8/12	Monday 10/14/12	Monday 10/13/12
Remembrance Day	Friday 11/11/11	Sunday 11/11/12	Monday 11/11/13	Tuesday 11/11/14
Christmas Day	Sunday 12/25/11	Tuesday 12/25/12	Wednesday 12/25/13	Thursday 12/25/14
Boxing Day	Monday 12/26/11	Wednesday 12/26/12	Thursday 12/26/13	Friday 12/26/14

---

2 Source: pch.gc.ca, www.timeanddate.com/

The following calendars are consistent with others published by multiple sources. However, individual resorts and exchange companies vary from these dates.

2011 – Friday Check-In

Week	Start Day	End Day	Week	Start Day	End Day
1	1/7/2011	1/14/2011	27	7/8/2011	7/15/2011
2	1/14/2011	1/21/2011	28	7/15/2011	7/22/2011
3	1/21/2011	1/28/2011	29	7/22/2011	7/29/2011
4	1/28/2011	2/4/2011	30	7/29/2011	8/5/2011
5	2/4/2011	2/11/2011	31	8/5/2011	8/12/2011
6	2/11/2011	2/18/2011	32	8/12/2011	8/19/2011
7	2/18/2011	2/25/2011	33	8/19/2011	8/26/2011
8	2/25/2011	3/4/2011	34	8/26/2011	9/2/2011
9	3/4/2011	3/11/2011	35	9/2/2011	9/9/2011
10	3/11/2011	3/18/2011	36	9/9/2011	9/16/2011
11	3/18/2011	3/25/2011	37	9/16/2011	9/23/2011
12	3/25/2011	4/1/2011	38	9/23/2011	9/30/2011
13	4/1/2011	4/8/2011	39	9/30/2011	10/7/2011
14	4/8/2011	4/15/2011	40	10/7/2011	10/14/2011
15	4/15/2011	4/22/2011	41	10/14/2011	10/21/2011
16	4/22/2011	4/29/2011	42	10/21/2011	10/28/2011
17	4/29/2011	5/6/2011	43	10/28/2011	11/4/2011
18	5/6/2011	5/13/2011	44	11/4/2011	11/11/2011
19	5/13/2011	5/20/2011	45	11/11/2011	11/18/2011
20	5/20/2011	5/27/2011	46	11/18/2011	11/25/2011
21	5/27/2011	6/3/2011	47	11/25/2011	12/2/2011
22	6/3/2011	6/10/2011	48	12/2/2011	12/9/2011
23	6/10/2011	6/17/2011	49	12/9/2011	12/16/2011
24	6/17/2011	6/24/2011	50	12/16/2011	12/23/2011
25	6/24/2011	7/1/2011	51	12/23/2011	12/30/2011
26	7/1/2011	7/8/2011	52	12/30/2011	1/6/2012

2011 – Saturday Check-In

Week	Start Day	End Day	Week	Start Day	End Day
1	1/8/2011	1/15/2011	27	7/9/2011	7/16/2011
2	1/15/2011	1/22/2011	28	7/16/2a011	7/23/2011
3	1/22/2011	1/29/2011	29	7/23/2011	7/30/2011
4	1/29/2011	2/5/2011	30	7/30/2011	8/6/2011
5	2/5/2011	2/12/2011	31	8/6/2011	8/13/2011
6	2/12/2011	2/19/2011	32	8/13/2011	8/20/2011
7	2/19/2011	2/26/2011	33	8/20/2011	8/27/2011
8	2/26/2011	3/5/2011	34	8/27/2011	9/3/2011
9	3/5/2011	3/12/2011	35	9/3/2011	9/10/2011
10	3/12/2011	3/19/2011	36	9/10/2011	9/17/2011
11	3/19/2011	3/26/2011	37	9/17/2011	9/24/2011
12	3/26/2011	4/2/2011	38	9/24/2011	10/1/2011
13	4/2/2011	4/9/2011	39	10/1/2011	10/8/2011
14	4/9/2011	4/16/2011	40	10/8/2011	10/15/2011
15	4/16/2011	4/23/2011	41	10/15/2011	10/22/2011
16	4/23/2011	4/30/2011	42	10/22/2011	10/29/2011
17	4/30/2011	5/7/2011	43	10/29/2011	11/5/2011
18	5/7/2011	5/14/2011	44	11/5/2011	11/12/2011
19	5/14/2011	5/21/2011	45	11/12/2011	11/19/2011
20	5/21/2011	5/28/2011	46	11/19/2011	11/26/2011
21	5/28/2011	6/4/2011	47	11/26/2011	12/3/2011
22	6/4/2011	6/11/2011	48	12/3/2011	12/10/2011
23	6/11/2011	6/18/2011	49	12/10/2011	12/17/2011
24	6/18/2011	6/25/2011	50	12/17/2011	12/24/2011
25	6/25/2011	7/2/2011	51	12/24/2011	12/31/2011
26	7/2/2011	7/9/2011	52	12/31/2011	1/7/2012

2011 – Sunday Check-In

Week	Start Day	End Day	Week	Start Day	End Day
1	1/9/2011	1/16/2011	27	7/10/2011	7/17/2011
2	1/16/2011	1/23/2011	28	7/17/2011	7/24/2011
3	1/23/2011	1/30/2011	29	7/24/2011	7/31/2011
4	1/30/2011	2/6/2011	30	7/31/2011	8/7/2011
5	2/6/2011	2/13/2011	31	8/7/2011	8/14/2011
6	2/13/2011	2/20/2011	32	8/14/2011	8/21/2011
7	2/20/2011	2/27/2011	33	8/21/2011	8/28/2011
8	2/27/2011	3/6/2011	34	8/28/2011	9/4/2011
9	3/6/2011	3/13/2011	35	9/4/2011	9/11/2011
10	3/13/2011	3/20/2011	36	9/11/2011	9/18/2011
11	3/20/2011	3/27/2011	37	9/18/2011	9/25/2011
12	3/27/2011	4/3/2011	38	9/25/2011	10/2/2011
13	4/3/2011	4/10/2011	39	10/2/2011	10/9/2011
14	4/10/2011	4/17/2011	40	10/9/2011	10/16/2011
15	4/17/2011	4/24/2011	41	10/16/2011	10/23/2011
16	4/24/2011	5/1/2011	42	10/23/2011	10/30/2011
17	5/1/2011	5/8/2011	43	10/30/2011	11/6/2011
18	5/8/2011	5/15/2011	44	11/6/2011	11/13/2011
19	5/15/2011	5/22/2011	45	11/13/2011	11/20/2011
20	5/22/2011	5/29/2011	46	11/20/2011	11/27/2011
21	5/29/2011	6/5/2011	47	11/27/2011	12/4/2011
22	6/5/2011	6/12/2011	48	12/4/2011	12/11/2011
23	6/12/2011	6/19/2011	49	12/11/2011	12/18/2011
24	6/19/2011	6/26/2011	50	12/18/2011	12/25/2011
25	6/26/2011	7/3/2011	51	12/25/2011	1/1/2012
26	7/3/2011	7/10/2011	52	1/1/2012	1/8/2012

2012 – Friday Check-In

Week	Start Day	End Day	Week	Start Day	End Day
1	1/6/2012	1/13/2012	27	7/6/2012	7/13/2012
2	1/13/2012	1/20/2012	28	7/13/2012	7/20/2012
3	1/20/2012	1/27/2012	29	7/20/2012	7/27/2012
4	1/27/2012	2/3/2012	30	7/27/2012	8/3/2012
5	2/3/2012	2/10/2012	31	8/3/2012	8/10/2012
6	2/10/2012	2/17/2012	32	8/10/2012	8/17/2012
7	2/17/2012	2/24/2012	33	8/17/2012	8/24/2012
8	2/24/2012	3/2/2012	34	8/24/2012	8/31/2012
9	3/2/2012	3/9/2012	35	8/31/2012	9/7/2012
10	3/9/2012	3/16/2012	36	9/7/2012	9/14/2012
11	3/16/2012	3/23/2012	37	9/14/2012	9/21/2012
12	3/23/2012	3/30/2012	38	9/21/2012	9/28/2012
13	3/30/2012	4/6/2012	39	9/28/2012	10/5/2012
14	4/6/2012	4/13/2012	40	10/5/2012	10/12/2012
15	4/13/2012	4/20/2012	41	10/12/2012	10/19/2012
16	4/20/2012	4/27/2012	42	10/19/2012	10/26/2012
17	4/27/2012	5/4/2012	43	10/26/2012	11/2/2012
18	5/4/2012	5/11/2012	44	11/2/2012	11/9/2012
19	5/11/2012	5/18/2012	45	11/9/2012	11/16/2012
20	5/18/2012	5/25/2012	46	11/16/2012	11/23/2012
21	5/25/2012	6/1/2012	47	11/23/2012	11/30/2012
22	6/1/2012	6/8/2012	48	11/30/2012	12/7/2012
23	6/8/2012	6/15/2012	49	12/7/2012	12/14/2012
24	6/15/2012	6/22/2012	50	12/14/2012	12/21/2012
25	6/22/2012	6/29/2012	51	12/21/2012	12/28/2012
26	6/29/2012	7/6/2012	52	12/28/2012	1/4/2013

2012 – Saturday Check-In

Week	Start Day	End Day	Week	Start Day	End Day
1	1/7/2012	1/14/2012	27	7/7/2012	7/14/2012
2	1/14/2012	1/21/2012	28	7/14/2012	7/21/2012
3	1/21/2012	1/28/2012	29	7/21/2012	7/28/2012
4	1/28/2012	2/4/2012	30	7/28/2012	8/4/2012
5	2/4/2012	2/11/2012	31	8/4/2012	8/11/2012
6	2/11/2012	2/18/2012	32	8/11/2012	8/18/2012
7	2/18/2012	2/25/2012	33	8/18/2012	8/25/2012
8	2/25/2012	3/3/2012	34	8/25/2012	9/1/2012
9	3/3/2012	3/10/2012	35	9/1/2012	9/8/2012
10	3/10/2012	3/17/2012	36	9/8/2012	9/15/2012
11	3/17/2012	3/24/2012	37	9/15/2012	9/22/2012
12	3/24/2012	3/31/2012	38	9/22/2012	9/29/2012
13	3/31/2012	4/7/2012	39	9/29/2012	10/6/2012
14	4/7/2012	4/14/2012	40	10/6/2012	10/13/2012
15	4/14/2012	4/21/2012	41	10/13/2012	10/20/2012
16	4/21/2012	4/28/2012	42	10/20/2012	10/27/2012
17	4/28/2012	5/5/2012	43	10/27/2012	11/3/2012
18	5/5/2012	5/12/2012	44	11/3/2012	11/10/2012
19	5/12/2012	5/19/2012	45	11/10/2012	11/17/2012
20	5/19/2012	5/26/2012	46	11/17/2012	11/24/2012
21	5/26/2012	6/2/2012	47	11/24/2012	12/1/2012
22	6/2/2012	6/9/2012	48	12/1/2012	12/8/2012
23	6/9/2012	6/16/2012	49	12/8/2012	12/15/2012
24	6/16/2012	6/23/2012	50	12/15/2012	12/22/2012
25	6/23/2012	6/30/2012	51	12/22/2012	12/29/2012
26	6/30/2012	7/7/2012	52	12/29/2012	1/5/2013

2012 – Sunday Check-In

Week	Start Day	End Day	Week	Start Day	End Day
1	1/8/2012	1/15/2012	27	7/8/2012	7/15/2012
2	1/15/2012	1/22/2012	28	7/15/2012	7/22/2012
3	1/22/2012	1/29/2012	29	7/22/2012	7/29/2012
4	1/29/2012	2/5/2012	30	7/29/2012	8/5/2012
5	2/5/2012	2/12/2012	31	8/5/2012	8/12/2012
6	2/12/2012	2/19/2012	32	8/12/2012	8/19/2012
7	2/19/2012	2/26/2012	33	8/19/2012	8/26/2012
8	2/26/2012	3/4/2012	34	8/26/2012	9/2/2012
9	3/4/2012	3/11/2012	35	9/2/2012	9/9/2012
10	3/11/2012	3/18/2012	36	9/9/2012	9/16/2012
11	3/18/2012	3/25/2012	37	9/16/2012	9/23/2012
12	3/25/2012	4/1/2012	38	9/23/2012	9/30/2012
13	4/1/2012	4/8/2012	39	9/30/2012	10/7/2012
14	4/8/2012	4/15/2012	40	10/7/2012	10/14/2012
15	4/15/2012	4/22/2012	41	10/14/2012	10/21/2012
16	4/22/2012	4/29/2012	42	10/21/2012	10/28/2012
17	4/29/2012	5/6/2012	43	10/28/2012	11/4/2012
18	5/6/2012	5/13/2012	44	11/4/2012	11/11/2012
19	5/13/2012	5/20/2012	45	11/11/2012	11/18/2012
20	5/20/2012	5/27/2012	46	11/18/2012	11/25/2012
21	5/27/2012	6/3/2012	47	11/25/2012	12/2/2012
22	6/3/2012	6/10/2012	48	12/2/2012	12/9/2012
23	6/10/2012	6/17/2012	49	12/9/2012	12/16/2012
24	6/17/2012	6/24/2012	50	12/16/2012	12/23/2012
25	6/24/2012	7/1/2012	51	12/23/2012	12/30/2012
26	7/1/2012	7/8/2012	52	12/30/2012	1/6/2013

2013 – Friday Check-In

Week	Start Day	End Day	Week	Start Day	End Day
1	1/4/2013	1/11/2013	27	7/5/2013	7/12/2013
2	1/11/2013	1/18/2013	28	7/12/2013	7/19/2013
3	1/18/2013	1/25/2013	29	7/19/2013	7/26/2013
4	1/25/2013	2/1/2013	30	7/26/2013	8/2/2013
5	2/1/2013	2/8/2013	31	8/2/2013	8/9/2013
6	2/8/2013	2/15/2013	32	8/9/2013	8/16/2013
7	2/15/2013	2/22/2013	33	8/16/2013	8/23/2013
8	2/22/2013	3/1/2013	34	8/23/2013	8/30/2013
9	3/1/2013	3/8/2013	35	8/30/2013	9/6/2013
10	3/8/2013	3/15/2013	36	9/6/2013	9/13/2013
11	3/15/2013	3/22/2013	37	9/13/2013	9/20/2013
12	3/22/2013	3/29/2013	38	9/20/2013	9/27/2013
13	3/29/2013	4/5/2013	39	9/27/2013	10/4/2013
14	4/5/2013	4/12/2013	40	10/4/2013	10/11/2013
15	4/12/2013	4/19/2013	41	10/11/2013	10/18/2013
16	4/19/2013	4/26/2013	42	10/18/2013	10/25/2013
17	4/26/2013	5/3/2013	43	10/25/2013	11/1/2013
18	5/3/2013	5/10/2013	44	11/1/2013	11/8/2013
19	5/10/2013	5/17/2013	45	11/8/2013	11/15/2013
20	5/17/2013	5/24/2013	46	11/15/2013	11/22/2013
21	5/24/2013	5/31/2013	47	11/22/2013	11/29/2013
22	5/31/2013	6/7/2013	48	11/29/2013	12/6/2013
23	6/7/2013	6/14/2013	49	12/6/2013	12/13/2013
24	6/14/2013	6/21/2013	50	12/13/2013	12/20/2013
25	6/21/2013	6/28/2013	51	12/20/2013	12/27/2013
26	6/28/2013	7/5/2013	52	12/27/2013	1/3/2014

2013 – Saturday Check-In

Week	Start Day	End Day	Week	Start Day	End Day
1	1/5/2013	1/12/2013	27	7/6/2013	7/13/2013
2	1/12/2013	1/19/2013	28	7/13/2013	7/20/2013
3	1/19/2013	1/26/2013	29	7/20/2013	7/27/2013
4	1/26/2013	2/2/2013	30	7/27/2013	8/3/2013
5	2/2/2013	2/9/2013	31	8/3/2013	8/10/2013
6	2/9/2013	2/16/2013	32	8/10/2013	8/17/2013
7	2/16/2013	2/23/2013	33	8/17/2013	8/24/2013
8	2/23/2013	3/2/2013	34	8/24/2013	8/31/2013
9	3/2/2013	3/9/2013	35	8/31/2013	9/7/2013
10	3/9/2013	3/16/2013	36	9/7/2013	9/14/2013
11	3/16/2013	3/23/2013	37	9/14/2013	9/21/2013
12	3/23/2013	3/30/2013	38	9/21/2013	9/28/2013
13	3/30/2013	4/6/2013	39	9/28/2013	10/5/2013
14	4/6/2013	4/13/2013	40	10/5/2013	10/12/2013
15	4/13/2013	4/20/2013	41	10/12/2013	10/19/2013
16	4/20/2013	4/27/2013	42	10/19/2013	10/26/2013
17	4/27/2013	5/4/2013	43	10/26/2013	11/2/2013
18	5/4/2013	5/11/2013	44	11/2/2013	11/9/2013
19	5/11/2013	5/18/2013	45	11/9/2013	11/16/2013
20	5/18/2013	5/25/2013	46	11/16/2013	11/23/2013
21	5/25/2013	6/1/2013	47	11/23/2013	11/30/2013
22	6/1/2013	6/8/2013	48	11/30/2013	12/7/2013
23	6/8/2013	6/15/2013	49	12/7/2013	12/14/2013
24	6/15/2013	6/22/2013	50	12/14/2013	12/21/2013
25	6/22/2013	6/29/2013	51	12/21/2013	12/28/2013
26	6/29/2013	7/6/2013	52	12/28/2013	1/4/2014

2013 – Sunday Check-In

Week	Start Day	End Day	Week	Start Day	End Day
1	1/6/2013	1/13/2013	27	7/7/2013	7/14/2013
2	1/13/2013	1/20/2013	28	7/14/2013	7/21/2013
3	1/20/2013	1/27/2013	29	7/21/2013	7/28/2013
4	1/27/2013	2/3/2013	30	7/28/2013	8/4/2013
5	2/3/2013	2/10/2013	31	8/4/2013	8/11/2013
6	2/10/2013	2/17/2013	32	8/11/2013	8/18/2013
7	2/17/2013	2/24/2013	33	8/18/2013	8/25/2013
8	2/24/2013	3/3/2013	34	8/25/2013	9/1/2013
9	3/3/2013	3/10/2013	35	9/1/2013	9/8/2013
10	3/10/2013	3/17/2013	36	9/8/2013	9/15/2013
11	3/17/2013	3/24/2013	37	9/15/2013	9/22/2013
12	3/24/2013	3/31/2013	38	9/22/2013	9/29/2013
13	3/31/2013	4/7/2013	39	9/29/2013	10/6/2013
14	4/7/2013	4/14/2013	40	10/6/2013	10/13/2013
15	4/14/2013	4/21/2013	41	10/13/2013	10/20/2013
16	4/21/2013	4/28/2013	42	10/20/2013	10/27/2013
17	4/28/2013	5/5/2013	43	10/27/2013	11/3/2013
18	5/5/2013	5/12/2013	44	11/3/2013	11/10/2013
19	5/12/2013	5/19/2013	45	11/10/2013	11/17/2013
20	5/19/2013	5/26/2013	46	11/17/2013	11/24/2013
21	5/26/2013	6/2/2013	47	11/24/2013	12/1/2013
22	6/2/2013	6/9/2013	48	12/1/2013	12/8/2013
23	6/9/2013	6/16/2013	49	12/8/2013	12/15/2013
24	6/16/2013	6/23/2013	50	12/15/2013	12/22/2013
25	6/23/2013	6/30/2013	51	12/22/2013	12/29/2013
26	6/30/2013	7/7/2013	52	12/29/2013	1/5/2014

2014 – Friday Check-In

Week	Start Day	End Day	Week	Start Day	End Day
1	1/3/2014	1/10/2014	27	7/4/2014	7/11/2014
2	1/10/2014	1/17/2014	28	7/11/2014	7/18/2014
3	1/17/2014	1/24/2014	29	7/18/2014	7/25/2014
4	1/24/2014	1/31/2014	30	7/25/2014	8/1/2014
5	1/31/2014	2/7/2014	31	8/1/2014	8/8/2014
6	2/7/2014	2/14/2014	32	8/8/2014	8/15/2014
7	2/14/2014	2/21/2014	33	8/15/2014	8/22/2014
8	2/21/2014	2/28/2014	34	8/22/2014	8/29/2014
9	2/28/2014	3/7/2014	35	8/29/2014	9/5/2014
10	3/7/2014	3/14/2014	36	9/5/2014	9/12/2014
11	3/14/2014	3/21/2014	37	9/12/2014	9/19/2014
12	3/21/2014	3/28/2014	38	9/19/2014	9/26/2014
13	3/28/2014	4/4/2014	39	9/26/2014	10/3/2014
14	4/4/2014	4/11/2014	40	10/3/2014	10/10/2014
15	4/11/2014	4/18/2014	41	10/10/2014	10/17/2014
16	4/18/2014	4/25/2014	42	10/17/2014	10/24/2014
17	4/25/2014	5/2/2014	43	10/24/2014	10/31/2014
18	5/2/2014	5/9/2014	44	10/31/2014	11/7/2014
19	5/9/2014	5/16/2014	45	11/7/2014	11/14/2014
20	5/16/2014	5/23/2014	46	11/14/2014	11/21/2014
21	5/23/2014	5/30/2014	47	11/21/2014	11/28/2014
22	5/30/2014	6/6/2014	48	11/28/2014	12/5/2014
23	6/6/2014	6/13/2014	49	12/5/2014	12/12/2014
24	6/13/2014	6/20/2014	50	12/12/2014	12/19/2014
25	6/20/2014	6/27/2014	51	12/19/2014	12/26/2014
26	6/27/2014	7/4/2014	52	12/26/2014	1/2/2015

2014 – Saturday Check-In

Week	Start Day	End Day	Week	Start Day	End Day
1	1/4/2014	1/11/2014	27	7/5/2014	7/12/2014
2	1/11/2014	1/18/2014	28	7/12/2014	7/19/2014
3	1/18/2014	1/25/2014	29	7/19/2014	7/26/2014
4	1/25/2014	2/1/2014	30	7/26/2014	8/2/2014
5	2/1/2014	2/8/2014	31	8/2/2014	8/9/2014
6	2/8/2014	2/15/2014	32	8/9/2014	8/16/2014
7	2/15/2014	2/22/2014	33	8/16/2014	8/23/2014
8	2/22/2014	3/1/2014	34	8/23/2014	8/30/2014
9	3/1/2014	3/8/2014	35	8/30/2014	9/6/2014
10	3/8/2014	3/15/2014	36	9/6/2014	9/13/2014
11	3/15/2014	3/22/2014	37	9/13/2014	9/20/2014
12	3/22/2014	3/29/2014	38	9/20/2014	9/27/2014
13	3/29/2014	4/5/2014	39	9/27/2014	10/4/2014
14	4/5/2014	4/12/2014	40	10/4/2014	10/11/2014
15	4/12/2014	4/19/2014	41	10/11/2014	10/18/2014
16	4/19/2014	4/26/2014	42	10/18/2014	10/25/2014
17	4/26/2014	5/3/2014	43	10/25/2014	11/1/2014
18	5/3/2014	5/10/2014	44	11/1/2014	11/8/2014
19	5/10/2014	5/17/2014	45	11/8/2014	11/15/2014
20	5/17/2014	5/24/2014	46	11/15/2014	11/22/2014
21	5/24/2014	5/31/2014	47	11/22/2014	11/29/2014
22	5/31/2014	6/7/2014	48	11/29/2014	12/6/2014
23	6/7/2014	6/14/2014	49	12/6/2014	12/13/2014
24	6/14/2014	6/21/2014	50	12/13/2014	12/20/2014
25	6/21/2014	6/28/2014	51	12/20/2014	12/27/2014
26	6/28/2014	7/5/2014	52	12/27/2014	1/3/2015

2014 – Sunday Check-In

Week	Start Day	End Day	Week	Start Day	End Day
1	1/5/2014	1/12/2014	27	7/6/2014	7/13/2014
2	1/12/2014	1/19/2014	28	7/13/2014	7/20/2014
3	1/19/2014	1/26/2014	29	7/20/2014	7/27/2014
4	1/26/2014	2/2/2014	30	7/27/2014	8/3/2014
5	2/2/2014	2/9/2014	31	8/3/2014	8/10/2014
6	2/9/2014	2/16/2014	32	8/10/2014	8/17/2014
7	2/16/2014	2/23/2014	33	8/17/2014	8/24/2014
8	2/23/2014	3/2/2014	34	8/24/2014	8/31/2014
9	3/2/2014	3/9/2014	35	8/31/2014	9/7/2014
10	3/9/2014	3/16/2014	36	9/7/2014	9/14/2014
11	3/16/2014	3/23/2014	37	9/14/2014	9/21/2014
12	3/23/2014	3/30/2014	38	9/21/2014	9/28/2014
13	3/30/2014	4/6/2014	39	9/28/2014	10/5/2014
14	4/6/2014	4/13/2014	40	10/5/2014	10/12/2014
15	4/13/2014	4/20/2014	41	10/12/2014	10/19/2014
16	4/20/2014	4/27/2014	42	10/19/2014	10/26/2014
17	4/27/2014	5/4/2014	43	10/26/2014	11/2/2014
18	5/4/2014	5/11/2014	44	11/2/2014	11/9/2014
19	5/11/2014	5/18/2014	45	11/9/2014	11/16/2014
20	5/18/2014	5/25/2014	46	11/16/2014	11/23/2014
21	5/25/2014	6/1/2014	47	11/23/2014	11/30/2014
22	6/1/2014	6/8/2014	48	11/30/2014	12/7/2014
23	6/8/2014	6/15/2014	49	12/7/2014	12/14/2014
24	6/15/2014	6/22/2014	50	12/14/2014	12/21/2014
25	6/22/2014	6/29/2014	51	12/21/2014	12/28/2014
26	6/29/2014	7/6/2014	52	12/28/2014	1/4/2015

Glossary and Acronyms List

The following terms and acronyms are defined within the context of timeshares:

AC	Accommodation Certificate
Accommodation Certificate (AC)	bonus week coupons offered by Interval International for high value exchange deposits
affiliated exchange company	an exchange company that makes contractual arrangements to interact with a particular timeshare resort or system to support owners that want to exchange their use time
ARDA	American Resort Development Association
assignment	conveying your right to use your unit to someone else for a particular year (either for free or in return for rent)
banking	ceding control over your unit to an exchange company in return for the promise of another week – transfers right to use
basis	cost value at time of purchase or conversion used to calculate profit or loss
biennial	Right to use a timeshare every other year instead of annually. Owners may have access on even years or odd years.
broker	intermediary who represents seller in a timeshare purchase transaction
CARE	Cooperative Association of Resort Exchangers
charter buyer	a person who buys their week from the developer as an original owner
check-in day	day of the week when use starts for a particular timeshare
closing	final step in a timeshare purchase transaction

condo docs	condominium documents which vary by state and identify rules and regulations of the timeshare
Covenants	written agreement documenting the timeshare rules
CPA	Certified Public Accountant
deed	signed, legal written document conveying title of a timeshare from a grantor to a grantee
deed in lieu	conveying ownership to HOA instead of paying owed maintenance fees and special assessments
deposit first	approach to exchanging in which a week is banked prior to searching for an exchange
depositing	see banking
depreciation	decline in timeshare ownership value
developer	the company that builds the resort and sells to charter owners
direct exchange	trading the use of weeks directly with another owner without the use of an exchange company
dues	like maintenance fees at vacation clubs
EOY	every other year
exchange company	an independent organization that helps timeshare owners trade their rights to access their unit for a comparable unit at a different time and place
exchanging	trading your right to use in return for right to use someone else's week
EY	every year
Fair Market Value (FMV)	price the timeshare would sell for on the resale market
fee-simple deed	document used to convey title
fixed week	ownership rights associated with a particular week of the year beginning on a particular day of the week
floating week	varying access vice a fixed week – subject to availability; ownership rights that allow choice of week
FMV	fair market value

foreclosure	legal process in which a lien holder (usually a lender or the resort) obtains ownership of a timeshare due to money owed (e.g., nonpayment of loan or maintenance fees)
fractional ownership	often refers to a timeshare model with a longer access period than a week
Getaway	II rentals available to II members
Gold Crown	RCI's highest quality designation
HOA	Home Owners Association
Homeowner Association (HOA)	organization that represents owners and makes decisions regarding management and budget
home resort	resort where week is owned, may be used to establish reservation-making window and maintenance fee calculations
II	Interval International
Interval International (II)	assisted exchange company
Last Call	RCI name for weeks that are deposited or made available by the resort shortly before they're available and are offered for discounted rental prices
leasehold	ownership of building on rented land
letter of declination	document showing that the resort is waiving their right of first refusal (ROFR)
light red	second highest ranking of timeshare weeks
limited kitchen	II term for kitchen without a full size refrigerator, stove, and oven
Limited Liability Company (LLC)	a type of corporate entity that might shield owners from negative consequences associated with foreclosure
LLC	Limited Liability Company
lock-off unit	unit layout that allows for separating with locked doors allowing for multiple weeks of use or exchange
Maintenance Fees (MF)	owner's portion of expenses associated with resort upkeep and management

MF	Maintenance Fees
mud season	low season at ski resorts
National Timeshare Owners Association (NTOA)	consumer advocacy organization for timeshare owners
NTOA	National Timeshare Owners Association
opportunity costs	loss of use of funds from purchase price being tied up
PCC	Postcard Company
point system	timeshare ownership model that uses points
point conversion	exchanging deeded ownership week for a set number of points in a point system
points	relative value of ownership used to determine equitable access or exchange
points-based management company	company contracted by the owning entity or the owning entity itself that manages the points system
points conversion	the process of changing a deeded ownership into a points-based system
pool	group of weeks (or the place where you go swimming)
Postcard Company (PCC)	a company that advertises (often using postcards sent to timeshare owners) that claims they can help sell a timeshare (often for an up-front fee without any guarantee of success
program documents	documents describing a particular timeshare plan and HOA's operation
property	the specific physical location of a resort
quitclaim deed	legal document that disclaims interest in a timeshare and grants ownership claims to someone else
RCI	assisted exchange company
RCI Points	point program administered by RCI
RCI Weeks	RCI's exchange program
red week	designation for most desirable weeks

Redweek.com	online timeshare sales and rental company
request first	approach to exchange where request is made prior to a week being banked
resale week	week sold by someone other than developer
rescission	cancelling a timeshare purchase through the process dictated by the state and the purchase documents
rescission period	the timeframe within which a buyer can rescind (see rescission)
resort	physical property where owners access their unit; also used to refer to HOA or managing company
retail timeshare purchase	buying from developer
Right of First Refusal (ROFR)	developer's ability to repurchase ownership being sold by an owner
right of rescission	(see rescission)
Right to Use (RTU) system	access model that provides a set number of years of access (term) – usually without a deed
ROFR	Right of First Refusal
RTU	Right to Use
SA	Special Assessment
season	group of weeks
Silver Crown	RCI's second highest quality designation
sniping	auction strategy of making last minute bids
Special Assessment (SA)	fee paid by owners for unanticipated expense
survey	set of questions for scoring the quality of a timeshare resort
swing week	floating week
term	time period of RTU membership
tidy service	limited mid-week cleaning
tiger trader	week with a very high exchange value
timeshare	approach for sharing resort real estate with weekly intervals

timeshare calendar	list of weeks for each year indicating check-in/check-out date for each week and check-in day of week
timeshare plan	official document filed by a timeshare developer with the state
Timeshare User's Group (TUG)	online resource providing consumer information about timeshares
trading power	value a particular week has for exchange purposes – tied to exchange company's internal formulas; relative value of a week being exchanged based on supply and demand
trial membership	option for sampling a timeshare for a designated period of time
TUG	Timeshare User's Group
unit	the particular suite at a resort assigned to the owner, exchanger, tenant, or guest
uptrading	exchanging for a better week
used timeshare	timeshare owner bought as a resale rather than directly from a developer
Vacation Club (VC)	timeshare approach that provides members with access, often using a points based approach
VC	vacation club
warranty deed	deed where owners guarantee or "warrant" rights
week	assigned time period at a resort; timeshare ownership
yellow week/ season	less valuable/desirable week than red or light red week